THE
EIGHTH
ROUND

Punch Out
Publishing

THE

EIGHTH

ROUND

A True Story

by

Zeke Wilson

The Eighth Round

Copyright © 2005, 2009 Zeke Wilson

All Rights Reserved.

For rights and permissions information, contact:
Punch Out Publishing
Administrative Office
all@punchoutpublishing.com

Visit us online at www.punchoutpublishing.com

ISBN   0-9825174-0-8

ISBN-13   978-0-9825174-0-6

Author's Note:
This is a work of non-fiction. Some names
of persons and places may have been changed
in order to protect the privacy of persons involved.

TABLE OF CONTENTS

DEDICATION

This book is dedicated to
my Mother, Florence H. Wilson,
who instilled in me the will
to persevere in all things;

To my sister Frenisee Wilson,
who inspired me to
reach beyond my limits;

And universally to
all Mothers everywhere,
whose lives are a monument
to helping all children
reach their full potential.

"There are those who say to you – we are rushing this issue of civil rights. I say we are 172 years late."
Hubert H. Humphrey
Speech at Democratic National Convention, July 14, 1948

"I'm the world's original gradualist. I just think ninety-odd years is gradual enough." -- Thurgood Marshall
May 19, 1958, referring to Dwight Eisenhower's call for patience regarding the progress of civil rights.

"If a man hasn't discovered something he will die for, he isn't fit to live." Rev. Dr. Martin Luther King, Jr.
June 23, 1963, Speech in Detroit.

"I have a dream that one day this nation will rise up and live out the true meaning of its creed: 'We hold these truths to be self-evident, that all men are created equal.'"
Rev. Dr. Martin Luther King, Jr.
August 28, 1963, Speech at Civil Rights March on Washington.

"Change will not come if we wait for some other person or some other time. We are the ones we've been waiting for. We are the change that we seek." -- Barack Obama
Speech, Feb. 5, 2008

PREFACE

It has now been a few years since the events in this story occurred. I have felt compelled to tell my story with the hope and intent that it will inspire and empower people to recognize injustice and oppression in their everyday lives, give them the resolve to weed it out and pull it up by its roots.

I believe in the American justice system. The

legislative and judicial branches of our government are designed in such a way that they are living, growing things. Like children, they are not perfect, but are growing and forming every day. Should we want justice, it is our duty to help shape it by demonstrating no tolerance for injustice. If we want equality under the law, we have a duty to be actively involved in shaping the laws that effect our lives.

Most importantly, we need to guard against apathy. Granted, it is always easier to accept the status quo than to change it, but ease should not be our primary resolve.

If we want future generations to enjoy true freedom and equality, we must fight now to wipe out injustice at every level. We cannot resort to violent means. We cannot resort to fostering hatred. We cannot teach our children either to accept the injustice or to hate its perpetrators, but to take a positive and active stance in ensuring that the future of the American people is one characterized by equality of opportunity for every single person who calls himself or herself American— regardless of color, race, ancestry, belief, or lifestyle preference.

It is my fervent desire to encourage every **person** to replace excuses with action. If you lack education, know and accept that you have the capacity to educate yourself. Make informed decisions. Ask questions. Use reason. Become self-educated, and you will possess knowledge and understanding that are truly your own.

If you lack money, re-prioritize. I speak from experience, having existed at various levels of the American dream. Accept that I fought this battle without the funds that everyone told me were necessary. I found truth in the principle outlined by our first Statesmen—that Justice in America must be available to all, or it is useful to none. Where money is scarce, education overcomes. Gone are the days when only the rich could afford justice. Our court system is available to all, with the prerequisite only that you are willing to learn the rules of court and the laws. If I did it, so can you.

Finally, don't give in to self-pity. People will only disempower you if you let them. Know that our founding fathers had a clear vision. Having come from a system of unequal access to the courts, they built steps to ensure we would not suffer the same future. Where those steps have become cracked, it is our duty to patch and rebuild them to serve their original purpose.

These duties are not ones that we can afford to ignore, unless we want future generations to live in a world without justice. So when you fight, fight for them. Build solid the steps of freedom and equality, and you will leave a legacy that will restore the title of "American" to its rightful place.

--Zeke Wilson
2009

"They that can give up essential liberty to obtain a little temporary safety deserve neither liberty nor safety. "
Benjamin Franklin
Historical Review of Pennsylvania, 1759

"I'm looking at the man in the mirror…I'm asking him to change his ways….And no message could have been any clearer—if you want to make the world a better place, take a look at **yourself,** and make the change."
Michael Jackson
In Memoriam, 1958-2009

"Hatred paralyzes life; love releases it.
Hatred confuses life; love harmonizes it.
Hatred darkens life; love illuminates it."
Rev. Dr. Martin Luther King, Jr.

INTRODUCTION

The hallway was meticulously clean, as always, despite the flow of traffic in and out of the courtrooms. Toward the bay was a wall constructed entirely of glass windows, reaching stories to let in light and the sights of the courtyard. In the distance, boats moved to and fro in the harbor, and the ferry made its regular runs.

I sat on a wooden bench in the hallway, watching

the movement in the bay. The wooden seats reminded me of pews, with their antique look and feel. After a week of trial, at least these were in the hallway. The trial had lasted an entire week, and I had spent a day and a half on the stand, followed by my witnesses and then the witnesses for the defense. I had spent the previous day at the same spot, waiting for the jury to finish deliberations, and was halfway through the morning and wondering how long the jurors would be.

The sound of giggling distracted me, and I looked toward the balcony where my wife and daughter, now six, were discussing the erratic flight patterns of the seagulls.

The balcony gave a view of the floor below, where Harry Miller sat in the cafeteria with his laptop, working steadily with frequent breaks to think. Many people told me that when it comes to constitutional issues, Harry is one of the best in the state. In fact, my initial contact with Harry had been years ago, but I just couldn't afford his retainer—even when he agreed to reduce it by more than half.

That wasn't Harry's fault. The fact is that at the time I could afford nothing over a few hundred dollars.

Less than a month before, Harry still hadn't been on the case. I was acting pro se, a difficult position to be in, given the fact that the Defendants were represented by the Massachusetts Attorney General's office. Of course, the alternative was to not pursue the issue, and that was not an option that I was about to entertain, having always been a fighter and knowing that if I did not fight for the constitutional rights that had been gained at such a struggle by so many people, their struggle would be lost amid a sea of "customary practices" that would negate every right that we all have to be treated equally.

And now, here I was, waiting for the jury to make a decision after reviewing thousands of pages of documentation and days of testimony.

At least it gave me time to think, time to reflect on the events in my life that lead to this point. Having been born in the Deep South, on Frogmore, an island close to Beaufort, South Carolina, in a time when the entire country but especially the South was undergoing so many changes, when the bounds of human consciousness were being redefined and civil rights waged an ongoing struggle.

Looking back, it seemed as if my entire life was in preparation for this moment, and these issues of equality and constitutional rights were ones that I began to realize I had been dealing with all of my life. My thoughts went back to my childhood, and to the key events that would help shape who I would become.

"We are confronted primarily with a moral
issue...whether all Americans are to be afforded equal
rights and equal opportunities, whether we are going to
treat our fellow Americans as we want to be treated."
John F. Kennedy, June 11, 1963, Referring to race riots in
Alabama in a radio broadcast.

"I am – Somebody. I may be poor, but I am –
Somebody! I may be on welfare, but I am – Somebody! I
may be uneducated, but I am – Somebody! I must be, I'm
God's child. I must be respected and protected. I am
black and I am beautiful! I am – Somebody!"
Jesse Jackson, 1966, Address to Operation Breadbasket rally.

"Kings or parliaments could not give the rights essential to happiness…We claim them for a higher source—from the King of kings, and Lord of all the earth. They are not annexed to us by parchments and seals. They are created in us by the decrees of Providence, which establish the laws of our nature. They are born with us; exist with us; and cannot be taken from us by any human power, without taking our lives." -- John Dickinson

"They (the founders) proclaimed to all the world the revolutionary doctrine of the divine rights of the common man. That doctrine has ever since been the heart of the American faith." -- Dwight D. Eisenhower

"A right is not what someone gives you; it's what no one can take from you." -- Ramsey Clark

"America did not invent human rights. In a very real sense, it is the other way around. Human rights invented America." -- Jimmy Carter

"Freedom and the power to choose should not be the privilege of wealth. They are the birthright of every American." -- George H. W. Bush

"You kids can do anything in life, anything at all,
if you work hard and keep in your mind what you want."
Florence H. Wilson
June 10, 1964, Wallace Plantation, Frogmore, SC

THE FIRST ROUND:

◆————————◆

EARLY CHILDHOOD

Mama was a hard worker, a good woman who was able to see her kids graduate high school, go off to college and the military, help raise numerous grandchildren, and never seemed to mind all of the hard work that her life required. I was born the seventh child in a household with an absent father.

Mama worked full time at the crab factory on the island for as long as I could remember. She wanted to leave her kids something more, so she instilled in us a will to go forward, to persevere and never give up. She would come home from her job, and then work in the fields most evenings until the sun was down. But she would always find time to teach all of her children important lessons and make sure we were being raised with the morals and values that we needed, and that we were all getting the best education that we could.

She taught us to be independent, but also to depend on each other. My memories were of a good childhood, but one filled with responsibility and hard work.

Mama often sat, rocking in a slow, rhythmic motion that seemed to accent her words, and spoke with me. These were the days before television, and evenings were family time.

She would use the opportunity to tell each of her children special thoughts about the time they were born, experiences during their early childhood, and family history. She knew that she had a difficult task, raising black children alone in a time that was in upheaval.

Perhaps if fate had located her in the North instead of the South, things would have been somewhat different. But, as it was, her family was born and raised in the South, and her children's history included slavery only five generations before theirs. For her, the issues were inescapable.

I sat, listening intently as Mama recounted the stormy days when I was just an infant. As a result, my appreciation for the struggles of many grew even as I was just a child.

For her seventh child, as with her others, she had special words. I was born in April of 1957, the year that President Eisenhower introduced his Civil Rights Act. The bill was introduced reluctantly by a President who was not known for supporting civil rights issues.

"It all started about the time you were born, in a town called Little Rock, Arkansas. Some folks there decided to send their black children to an all-white school," Mama started, pausing to make sure that she had my full attention.

"Can they do that?" I asked, my eyes wide. I couldn't imagine going to a white school, and integration had not yet reached us.

"Well, the law says that they can, but a lot of people don't want their schools to be mixed. So what happened was, people demanded that the government do something. You see, the nine black students were all set to begin in the all-white school. The day before their enrollment, their Governor ordered two hundred seventy National Guard troops to move into the high school. He felt that the troops were necessary to maintain order, because he said that there might be trouble," Mama took a deep breath before continuing.

I fidgeted, then whispered, "The kids had to be brave."

Nodding, Mama continued, "The school board asked the students not to show up—and they didn't, the first day. The second day, the students did go to school, with two white and two black ministers."

"And what happened, Mama?" I asked.

"People were shocked about the response when the students got to school. The state's National Guard troops refused to let them go in the school, and as they left, people were causing problems and calling the students all sorts of names."

I interrupted to ask, "Real bad names, Mama?"

Mama paused to explain, "I think so. This was a big argument. The federal government said that the schools had to accept the black students. The state was challenging the Federal government and their control over the state's right to make their own laws."

"Who's higher, Mama? The federal government or the state?" I wondered.

Mama replied, "The federal government. But the President of the United States said that he would not use Federal troops to enforce desegregation."

I interrupted. "What's desegregation?"

"That means taking all the white students in the white schools and the black students in the black schools and letting them go to school together, in whichever school is closer to their homes. One day, all schools will have black and white and all kinds of kids in them," explained Mama patiently, "So this was much bigger than nine students. This was about who would make the decisions, and people in power didn't want to take orders, they all wanted to give them."

"So what did they do?" I asked, staring up at Mama from my seat on the floor.

Mama continued, in a quiet voice, "The President

and the Governor had a meeting that lasted eighteen whole days. While that was happening, people were getting more and more upset."

"Was he a good President, Mama?" I interrupted again.

"I guess so. And finally," she continued, "the students' right to education was upheld."

She went on to explain, "A few weeks later, the nine students went back to school. They sneaked in through a back door to avoid the mobs at the main doors."

I couldn't hold back. "Wow!"

"When people found out that the students were inside the building, they got really mad. Black people were attacked in the street. So were the writers for the Northern newspapers who were there to record the news."

Worried, I asked, "Were the kids okay?"

"Yeah, some people managed to smuggle the kids safely out of the building, and the mayor called and asked the President for help. He ordered the mob to go home. When another hate group showed up the next day, he sent in paratroopers and took control of the

National Guard. This was the first time since the Civil War that federal troops had been sent to the South to help black citizens," Mama finished.

"Wow!" I sat, amazed that all of this was happening around the time I was born. I was even more amazed that there were already schools in the South with both black and white students.

The air was too hot to breathe. Mama didn't seem to notice, though, as she worked without hesitation in the row next to me. She had the kind of inner strength to raise six more growing kids. A young boy, I was tall and thin and used to field work. My familiarity with the feel of the sandy soil was already apparent as I worked at the speed of an adult. I wasn't alone. Three of my sisters and two of my brothers were scattered over a few rows in the unending fields.

Sensing an opportunity to instill some important lessons into her children, Mama began, "You kids can do anything in life. Anything at all. If you work hard, and keep in your mind what you want. . ." Her words combined with the sound of the breeze through the cotton plants and created a rhythm that was both comforting and secure.

The next morning was hectic, as usual. Mama hustled back and forth through the house, preparing for work. She hurried through the old but clean dining room, stopping only to place a single sheet of paper on the large wooden table before spotting the bus approaching through the dining room window. Mama always left a list of chores with Frenisee. At fourteen, she was the oldest at home.

"Frenisee?" Mama yelled as she gathered her purse and headed for the front door.

"Yes, Mama?" came the reply from the back of the house.

"I'm leaving for work. There's a list of chores on the table for the kids to do." Mama's voice trailed as the door closed behind her.

"Okay, Mama," Frenisee replied, mostly to herself, then, louder, "Kids, you'd better pull those weeds before the sun gets too hot!"

The five who were younger than Frenisee were responsible for field work every morning. Then the boys would feed the pigs and chickens that were kept for meat and eggs. There was wood to cut and split, and water to haul from the pump outside into the house.

After finishing their chores, there was time to play kickball. There wasn't much else for a seven-year-old on Wallace Plantation to do, but life was good. I loved to be outdoors, and would spend time in the woods behind the house, climbing trees and exploring imaginary places.

It was evening now. Mama had been home, traded her apron for a hoe and headed to the fields. When the sun set, the family returned to the house for dinner, and to listen to the radio. Mama took her normal seat on the large, wooden rocking chair next to the radio, mending a shirt. I sat on the floor, playing with my fire engine.

Just a few weeks earlier, at the end of June, the news told the story of an investigation that began with the burning of a church in Mississippi. A group of three civil rights workers who were campaigning for black voting rights turned up missing.

And now, the bodies of the three civil rights

workers were found. I listened intently to the distant voice of the radio announcer, as he droned on in an almost artificial voice.

"You'll remember that just three weeks ago, we reported an investigation that began with the burning of a church in Mississippi. A group of three civil rights workers who were campaigning for Negro voting rights were reported as missing. There is an update this evening. According to reports, the bodies of the three civil rights workers have now been found. A controversy continues into allegations that local law enforcement officers had detained the three, and that later the three boys were released into the hands of a group of Klan members."

At seven, the only white people I had contact with were John Trask and Mr. Sanders, who owned large farms nearby, and the family's insurance agent, Mr. Morris.

The events at the time prompted me to ask, "Mama, why would Americans kill other Americans?"

Her answer could not make sense, but she explained that hate sometimes makes people hurt others to try to keep an advantage over them, to "keep them down" where they are no threat. Mama explained that you can't grow with hate in your heart, without that hate eating away at you—and I never saw her do or say anything hateful, despite the times.

Times were very hard, but Mama kept the Lord in her heart, knowing that kind of hate was all around her. Keeping her kids safe and keeping them on the right path to do good things in life was her number-one priority. I remember going to school and listening to the other kids saying it was wrong for those white men to kill the three civil rights workers, who were only campaigning for Negro voting rights. Being a young boy, I did not understand a lot of what was going on.

Today felt different. There was electricity in the air, as excitement filled everyone on Wallace Plantation. Dr. Martin Luther King would be speaking today at Ebenezer Baptist, the community church where Mama took her children to attend services every Sunday. King was a man so respected by the community that no one would want to miss him. At nine, I understood that Dr. King was a great man who believed that his dream of equality was within reach for all people.

Everyone was buzzing around the house, getting ready. Soon Mr. Robert Parker would be getting there early to drive the family to the service. A deacon in the church, Mr. Parker became my godfather when he participated in my baptism. He would often sit and talk with me, and as my father was absent most of the time, he taught me so many important things that a boy needed to learn to be a young man. He taught me to be responsible and to get along with people. He also instilled in me a sense of community and the importance of education.

The excitement continued to grow as members of the community arrived at the church. Everyone wanted to make sure that they'd be able to hear Dr. King, and were arriving early for a seat or place to stand. The atmosphere was festive, as neighbors greeted each other with smiles glowing in anticipation of Dr. King's message.

I was amazed at the effect that Dr. King had on these people, people who I had known all of my life. Merely the anticipation of seeing and hearing King excited people, gave them hope and spread an attitude of peace and positive change.

Standing in the back of the church with my brothers and sisters, friends from school and children from nearby communities, I laughed and clapped, absorbing all of Dr. King's words. Even after hearing so much praise on the radio and from the adults in my life, I had only a limited understanding of the life-changing work being done by the young preacher.

That warm summer evening, I rode home with a group of kids on the back of my neighbor's pickup truck. I couldn't help but notice that the conversation among my friends, which normally centered on frivolous children's matters, this evening instead revolved around the values promoted by Dr. King.

"Injustice anywhere is a threat to justice everywhere. We are caught in an inescapable network of mutuality, tied in a single garment of destiny. Whatever affects one directly, affects all indirectly." -- Rev. Dr. Martin Luther King, Jr., April 16, 1963, Letter from Birmingham Jail.

"An individual who breaks a law that conscience tells him is unjust, and who willingly accepts the penalty of imprisonment in order to arouse the conscience of the community over its injustice, is in reality expressing the highest respect for the law."
Rev. Dr. Martin Luther King, Jr.

"But there is something that I must say to my people who stand on the warm threshold which leads into the palace of justice. In the process of gaining our rightful place we must not be guilty of wrongful deeds. Let us not seek to satisfy our thirst for freedom by drinking from the cup of bitterness and hatred. We must forever conduct our struggle on the high plane of dignity and discipline. We must not allow our creative protest to degenerate into physical violence. Again and again we must rise to the majestic heights of meeting physical force with soul force. The marvelous new militancy which has engulfed the Negro community must not lead us to distrust of all white people, for many of our white brothers, as evidenced by their presence here today, have come to realize that their destiny is tied up with our destiny and their freedom is inextricably bound to our freedom. We cannot walk alone...
When we let freedom ring, when we let it ring from every village and every hamlet, from every state and every city, we will be able to speed up that day when all of God's children, black men and white men, Jews and Gentiles, Protestants and Catholics, will be able to join hands and sing in the words of the old Negro spiritual, 'Free at last! Free at last!
Thank God Almighty, we are free at last!' "
Rev. Dr. Martin Luther King, Jr.,
August 28, 1963, I Have a Dream Speech, Washington, D.C.

THE SECOND ROUND:

———◆————◆———

TEENAGE YEARS

The summer ended quickly, and I found myself, like many others my age, accepting an after-school job working at Penn Center for a man named Mr. Leroy Brown. He taught us that to be successful in life, one would need to always do his best and to work as hard as he could.

I was thankful to be able to work with Mr. Brown. There was a shortage of jobs that were available to kids my age, but the school referred me and others as part of a program to assist the kids to learn important life skills.

The work was mainly agricultural. I especially enjoyed learning to operate the tractors. Most of my experience at home involved manual farming, and I recognized that these methods and my work with the horses were becoming obsolete.

On rainy days, I would return home and tell Mama, "We couldn't work outside today, so they had us doing inside work with the women." Inside work was never my favorite, but I learned to help sort mail and a variety of maintenance jobs.

Mr. Brown would always report well on my efforts. His report to the school and to Mama was always positive, and he would say, "One thing I can tell you, that Zeke is a hard worker. He's not afraid to exert himself."

Even while working at this job, I would often find myself thinking about what I wanted to do as a career, trying to figure out what I would do with my life.

◆————————◆

In the summer of '69, Mama received a phone call from a very good friend of the family, Ms. Seppie Dudley. An old widow and a former school teacher locally, she loved to talk about the importance of language arts and grammar. My brothers and sisters and I enjoyed working with her around her house.

She told Mama, "Mrs. Wilson, I'm so glad you'll grant permission and I feel your kids will enjoy the experience. So I'll leave it to you to give them the good news. Please call me if you have any questions."

I remember coming home from an afternoon baseball game, which we lost. Mama was smiling from the porch. We asked her what was up, and she told me and my brothers and sisters to sit down. She continued to say, "I had a phone call from Seppie Dudley, and Miss Dudley took the opportunity to arrange for all of you to appear as extras in a documentary called 'Forty Acres and a Mule' that will be filmed at Penn Center on St. Helena Island."

Needless to say, the Wilson children were ecstatic at the opportunity. I was amazed initially because of the pay--$45 a day--and I wondered how they could afford to pay so much and we were very excited about being in a movie. The film dealt with the end of the Civil War, and was a real learning experience.

In one segment, the slave owners were in a buggy and the children, as slaves in ragged clothes, were following on foot. I always remembered two characters in the buggy, a man and a woman, and would often quote their conversation.

"Mr. Filgrim," the woman would say, "you think more of the Negroes than they think of themselves."

"Not true, simply not true!" would be the response from the man. I also remembered walking behind the buggy and thinking that it was so unfair that the slaves, tired from the day's work, would walk behind the buggy that was carrying the white folks.

In another segment, we were doing fieldwork when a man rode into the field on horseback, announced freedom for the slaves and the end of the war, then fired a pistol into the air. The characters portraying the freed slaves celebrated, and ran out of the field.

In the third segment, my character was an army soldier in a Confederate uniform, leading injured and war-torn troops back home in a boat. I did not under-stand why my character would be fighting for the South, when the South was fighting to retain slavery.

But I learned a lot about racism that summer—how my ancestors five generations back were slaves, how it must have felt to be born into a life of being less than another person, with limited or no rights. I remembered thinking that I could not live like that, and was glad that I had been born into a time of equality— or so I thought.

◆———————◆

In 1970, my sister Mary and adopted sister Martha graduated in the final class of St. Helena High School. As a sign of the times, the new school year would open in the fall with the school renamed as St. Helena Junior High School, and grades ten through twelve would go to Beaufort High School.

More important than the name change was the fact that the new school year would find me returning to the eighth grade in an integrated school.

Needless to say, there was a good deal of racial tension. Nevertheless, I welcomed the change. Friends would sometimes ask me, "Zeke, how do you feel now that you'll be taking classes with white kids?"

Of course, I would always remember Mama's words, and I was really more concerned with the "important" issues. Like who I'd be sitting next to on the bus, wondering if I'd make friends with the new kids who'd be coming into the school, and wondering how my old friends would react to the changes. And if there would also be white teachers, and if I'd be able to get passing grades in my new classes.

There was not a time, that first year of integration, when the white and black students would mingle. Although The Powers That Be decided that the school would be integrated, there was so much tension and distrust that would take time to resolve.

At thirteen, I was already beginning to grow up, and Mama's years of training were beginning to show. Plus, I did make a lot of white friends that year, some of whom became close friends.

Still, integration was scary for me and my friends, it was uncharted water. It was not until this school year that I first heard the word "Nigger", other than on the television.

Thanks to Mama, I adjusted quickly. There were

many students, black and white, who had a much harder time adjusting to the fact that for the first time ever they were all being taught by the same teachers, sharing the same books and lunch room. They were all using the same locker rooms and taking gym class together.

I was always athletic and strong for my age. It's hard not to be physical when you begin farming at an early age, during a time when much of the work was done by hand. I was fourteen, and I sat with Mama one evening when everyone was relaxing. "Mama?" I began.

"Mmm hmm," Mama replied.

"I've been thinking about something," I said, pausing to check Mama's response before continuing, "It seems odd that nobody in our family has ever played football. The coach says he would like me to play, if it's okay with you."

It seemed like forever before Mama's brief reply. "As long as you can still finish your chores and your schoolwork, I'll let you play."

That year, I did play football for the St. Helena Panthers, and Coach Calvin White chose me to be the defensive captain.

Although the Panthers didn't win a single game that

year, my confidence grew by leaps and bounds because of the leadership that the Coach saw in me. I also learned that year that my future would <u>not</u> be in football. Although I was talented, the outcome of the game de-pended too much on the effort of the entire team.

Then, one day I saw an advertisement for the Ali/Frazier fight being held on March 8, 1971 at Madison Square Garden. Something clicked inside me, and I instantly took an interest in boxing. I asked Mama, "What would you think if I decided to become a prizefighter?" And her reply was, "It will take hard work, but everything you want to accomplish in life will take hard work."

My own experience in life was that everything was hard, so her words didn't scare me.

One day, I asked Mama how much a heavy bag would cost, even though I knew that every dime that was made on the farm and working in the fields, along with Mama's paycheck, was immediately consumed by bills and the cost of raising four growing kids still left at home.

So I spoke with Mr. Parker, and at my request, he

brought an empty feedbag, and I filled it with sand to use as a heavy bag. I took an axe and chopped down three trees for posts, dragged them home, dug holes for the posts and attached the third tree as a crossbeam, from which I hung my homemade heavy bag.

When the feedbag tore, I took an old pair of pants that I had outgrown the previous year, tied the legs together and filled the legs with sand. That lasted longer than the feedbag, and gave me my start in training.

After years of kickball, I confiscated the ball and made a speed bag by tying the ball tightly inside of an old shirt, and hung it from the crossbeam that was built for the heavy bag.

Each morning, I would get up at 4 AM and jog before school. My confidence continued to grow, and I began to train on my own.

When the new school year started, I still played football and neighborhood baseball, but they took second and third place to my first priority of boxing. Having gained my mother's consent, I was off and running.

"If you really want to do this, I'm behind you one

hundred percent!" she would say to me.

One day, while jogging home from Penn Center, a distance of about two miles, a Dodge Dart pulled up alongside me. The driver rolled down his window and asked me what I was doing.

"Working on my plans for the future," I replied.

"Are you a football player?" the man asked.

"Yes—but I have different plans," I began.

"And what is that?" asked the man.

"I would tell you, but you'd laugh."

Having received assurance that he would not laugh, I told the man that I wanted to be a prizefighter. The stranger kept his promise, and instead of laughing, he stopped his car and got out. "Maybe I can help you," he said.

He had my attention, so I stopped to listen. The gentleman explained that he worked at Penn Center, and asked me for my phone number, promising to keep in touch.

Giving him my phone number, I finished jogging home, and told Mama of the afternoon's events.

The next day, Macauley Washburn called. He was a businessman who could teach me how to get things done.   An educated man, Macauley spoke well and followed through on his promise to help. Over the weeks and months he became a significant role model and he also explained to me the business side of boxing, the roles of manager and trainer.

As he further explained, "Zeke, I'm too old to be a boxer, but not too old to help shape a young man's career through management and training." He and I sat many days in the yard behind Mama's house, talking about boxing and reviewing my morning's training. He also checked in with my younger sister Nellie, who became my timekeeper and would help keep me on track.

Across the bridge from Frogmore, about twelve or thirteen miles away, was Beaufort, South Carolina, the home of the Heavyweight Boxing Champion of the World, Joe Frazier. There was also a Marine Corps Air Station that had a boxing team. It was located just a few miles from Parris Island Marine Corps Recruit Depot.

Macauley used his contacts to arrange a trainer. Sgt. David Robinson, or "Top", as he was affectionately called, was a big man, always well groomed, and was a Career Marine. He had been a former USMC boxing champion and had a true love for the sport.

Top began to work with me, teaching me the basics, and would often comment at the speed with which I learned. Minors were not allowed on base, so Top would bring Marine boxers to my house to spar with me. With Nellie as timekeeper, we would often spar for hours, with Mama smiling in approval from the porch.

One afternoon, Macauley came to the house bringing good news. He arranged an amateur fight for me in Savannah, Georgia. I had never been to Savannah, but knew it was a big city. I couldn't wait to tell all of my friends.

The next two months flew by as we prepared both mentally and physically for my first amateur fight. I stepped up training, and had trouble focusing on anything else.

My friends were supportive, and told me that "first-time jitters" were normal. But I had none. I was ready!

My opponent was older and bigger, but Top taught me to train for his specific style. Still, I was at a disadvantage, because at twenty-two my opponent had been boxing in Savannah for a while and had much more experience than me.

The night of the fight, I was the third of three fighters that Top had fighting on the card. The first two were both Marines, and were my sparring partners back home. As the first ended his bout with a loss after a split decision, and then the second ended the same way, I reaffirmed my resolve to give everything that night to take home a victory.

I thought, "And here I am in Savannah, my opponent's hometown. I don't want this bout to end the way my sparring partners' did."

All of my friends were in the audience, as were family members and neighbors. I wasn't about to disappoint one of them.

As the referee gave his final instructions, I looked deeply into my opponent's eyes, knowing that my confidence level was up, and I was ready to get it on.

Then, the bell sounded and the first round began. The hard work paid off that night. I set a Georgia State Record for the fastest knockout, and the fight ended after ten seconds of the first round.

Promoter Joe Moody couldn't believe it. My family and friends were in awe. Top and Macauley were ecstatic. I was happy and relieved that I had accomplished my goal. The local newspaper printed the story, and suddenly everyone seemed to know what happened, and they congratulated me for weeks.

I continued to train and fight at every opportunity. A few months later, Top received orders to be transferred, and my heart felt empty in his absence. Of course, Macauley was still there, offering support and guidance, and he took over the task of arranging fights for me in cities like Brunswick, Hilton Head, Tampa, Savannah and other Southern cities.

I began to build an undefeated record, and was making quite a name for myself in the Amateur ranks. By the time I graduated from high school, I had already earned many honors in the boxing world. I took the South Carolina State Championship in 1975 in Hilton Head, South Carolina, by winning a tournament that ended in a decision in my favor. I also ended the year by winning the South Carolina State Golden Gloves.

FROGMORE BOXER IN ACTION
Zeke Wilson, local amateur boxer, will be in action Wednesday, August 28 in a heavyweight bout in Savannah. The 17-year-old Wilson will have a rematch with Jimmy Chumley who was knocked out in the first round of their first bout on June 26. The fight will be one of several which begins at 8 p.m. at the National Guard Armory on Eisenhower Drive in Savannah. (Photo by Bruce Welden)

In the spring of 1976, I was approaching the day that I would graduate from high school and faced a tough decision. I knew that although my heart was in boxing, I was at a point where I would not learn and grow from the competition that was available locally. I came to a point not uncommon to graduates when a decision about my future could not be procrastinated any further.

My choices were clear. I could stay at home, get a job locally and continue my amateur boxing career by fighting the local guys and probably do very well against them, or I could relocate to a city where there was more opportunity to further my boxing skills and career.

I consulted Macauley, who agreed that my opportunities would be limited if I stayed, and although he didn't really want me moving he knew that it would be in my best interest to do so. The decision where to go was not difficult.

The only person I knew of who was from Beaufort and made it in boxing was Joe Frazier, and Joe relocated to Philadelphia to further his boxing career. Since my oldest sister, Frenisee, was also living in Philadelphia, I decided to give her a call and ask for her opinion. She didn't hesitate to offer her home to me so that I would have time to settle in and check out Joe Frazier's boxing gym.

After considerable thought and many conversations with Mama and Frenisee, I made a decision. Only two weeks after graduation, I bought a train ticket that would take me to the famous fight city of Philadelphia.

Standing on the deck of the train station at Yemassee, South Carolina, I said my goodbyes to Mama and my sister Mary, who had come to see me off, and boarded the train with mixed feelings, but excited about going to a city where I could further my boxing career. During the twenty-one hour train ride, I had plenty of time to focus on my plans. Besides, the trip was made a little easier because my best friend from high school, Ricky Wright, had graduated the year before and had worked and waited a year, hoping that we could make the move together.

We arrived at Philadelphia's Thirtieth Street Station in the evening, and Frenisee was waiting, accompanied by her husband Ronald. She was happy that I was there, and I'm sure she recalled all those years as a child when she was responsible for all of her sisters and brothers.

It seemed that from my vantage point on the train, Philadelphia stretched on forever. Standing in Thirtieth Street Station, I was thinking, "Wow--Philadelphia is such a big city. I'm used to small cities like Savannah, Georgia, but this is a real big city."

After Ronald helped us with our luggage we walked toward the car, and went to South Philadelphia, to Frenisee and Ronald's house. The first thing I wanted to do was to go see Joe Frazier's gym. I was adamant about it. That was my reason for coming to Philadelphia. My brother-in-law suggested, "Why don't you get settled in and tomorrow morning I'll take you over to the gym and introduce you to the people who are there, and maybe you can apply for membership."

Despite suggestions that I spend some time visiting relatives who were awaiting my arrival, I was excited and didn't want to do anything or talk to anyone before going to the gym and see who was there.

Frenisee smiled knowingly. She remembered that on my prom night, Jimmy Young fought Muhammad Ali and I made my prom date wait until the television sportscast was over before we could leave for the prom. She wasn't surprised that I would let everything else wait; especially since she knew that Jimmy Young was one of the fighters who trained regularly at Clover Leaf, Joe Frazier's gym.

Ronald's first order of business the next morning was to take me to the gym, which was located at Broad and Glenwood on the North side of the city. I applied for membership and began training there right away.

At the gym, I was reunited with Charles Singleton, who had graduated from Beaufort a few years before. I was shocked, and our friendship made me feel like I was home again. I also made friends with Joe Frazier's son Marvis, who was a few years younger and still in school at the time.

I would train every day, and my brother-in-law taught me the subway route from Broad and Tasker to Broad and Glenwood on the Broad Street line. For a country boy, the subway was something new. At least I didn't ride alone; I made friends with a boxer named Randall "Tex" Cobb, who rode with me every day after training, and we became good friends. I kept in touch with Tex for years as he went on to become a major motion picture and television star.

At Frazier's gym, there were so many good fighters. I immediately recognized Jimmy Young as a top contender, the man who fought Muhammad Ali but lost a split decision. Duane Bobick was the silver medalist in the 1972 Olympic Games in Munich, Germany with a 32-0 pro record. Bennie Briscol was a middle-weight and ranked number one in the world. The number two ranked fighter who also worked out at Frazier's gym was Willie "The Worm" Monroe. Also, the 1976 Gold Medalist winners Leon and Michael Spinks worked out at the gym. These were only some of the people that trained at Joe Frazier's gym.

I found the excitement overwhelming. One day during the first week, I was there working with the heavy bag. I was approached by a young man named Willie Folks, who instantly recognized my potential and inquired about my training and ring experience. As I was watching Jimmy Young spar and was glued to his every move, Willie told me that I should be ready to spar with someone on Jimmy's level within six months.

That was one of my dreams and goals—to be able to spar with a top fighter like Jimmy Young. Willie had under-estimated my resolve, though, and only three weeks later I was offered my first sparring session with Jimmy.

I couldn't wait to get home and call Mama with the news. I could hear her voice swell with pride as she encouraged me to always do my best. My sister was equally happy and impressed.

I anxiously awaited the big day when I would step into the ring with Jimmy Young.

◆——————————◆

I remember walking into the gym one afternoon. Joe Frazier and George Benton were talking about Ron Lyles and the trouble he was in. Standing there, I listened to the conversation. They were looking for a good amateur heavyweight fighter to go into Rahway State Prison to work with Ron Lyles as a sparring partner.

George turned to me and asked, "Would you like to go into Rahway State Prison and box Ron Lyles in a five-round exhibition?"

I replied, "Yes, I would. *Absolutely.*"

The next day, I left Philadelphia en route to Elizabeth, New Jersey. Ron Lyles, like Jimmy Young,

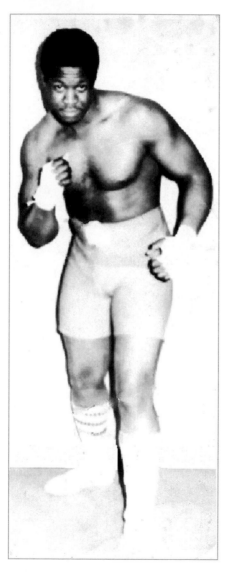

Zeke, age 20, in Joe Frazier's Gymnasium
Philadelphia, PA

was a top contender, and to box with him was one of the biggest things I had done in boxing, at that point. I got to box Ron Lyles in a five-round exhibition, and when I asked Ron how I did, he said, "Zeke, you are going to be a *very* good fighter." I thought about his comment all the way back to Philadelphia.

I was in Philadelphia for only two weeks when I found a job with a refrigeration company. I was accustomed to working and paying my way, and didn't want to become a burden on my sister or her family.

The work was okay, but I didn't like the way it interfered with my training schedule. The job was temporary, and when it ended, Ricky Wright's older brother, Chief, got me a job working for Crown Paper Company, recycling paper.

At Crown Paper, everyone worked a rotating shift. I juggled working and training as best I could, and soon sparring with Jimmy and other pro fighters became an everyday event. As excited as I was at first for the opportunity to be in the ring with fighters whom I felt had superior skills to mine, I soon began to realize that my skills were quickly approaching theirs.

I was both proud and excited when Joe Frazier invited me to become a member of his amateur boxing team. Soon afterwards, the team had the opportunity to participate in a boxing program with the inmates inside of Graterford State Penitentiary, and my brother-in-law accompanied me. The team did exceptionally well.

My days were focused on fitting my training schedule around my work schedule. Oftentimes, though, this meant that I would not get to spar with the fighters I wanted to, as their schedules were typically the same from day to day.

It was around the time when I started thinking, "I'm getting tired of working at a place that's not giving me the time to get to the gym and work with the guys that I like to work out with," when an incident occurred that caused me to consider making a change in my life.

While standing at the bus stop, waiting for the Septa bus, a police cruiser pulled up alongside the curb. The car was marked "K-9 Unit", which was unnecessary because as soon as the car came to a stop, the German Shepherd in the back began barking and lunging at the windows hard enough to shake the car. The officer rolled down the passenger window, and asked, "Hey, boy, what'cha doing here?"

"I'm waiting for the bus, officer," I replied.

"And where are you going?" he asked.

"To work, sir."

"You work?" he asked.

I looked nervously at the dog in the car, who seemed like he was about to come through the window.

"Yes, sir, officer.   At Crown Paper Company," I answered, after which the officer replied, "Where you from?"

"Sixth and McKean Street, sir."

The officer squinted and thought for a while, then asked, "How come I never saw you before?"

I explained that I moved there recently from the Carolinas.   The officer didn't look convinced, and by this time the dog was even more frantic than before.

"You see this dog?" he asked.   Without pausing for an answer, he continued, "Listen to me, boy, if I see you on this corner tomorrow, I'm gonna turn this dog loose. Do you hear me?"

I answered softly, "Yes, officer."

"Do you understand me?" he shouted.

I replied, a little louder, "Yes, sir."

After which he continued to ask, "Do I make myself clear?"

I tried to conceal the anger in my voice as I replied, "Yes, sir, you do."

As the police cruiser pulled slowly away and the bus pulled up to take me to work, I thought that it was a shame that the officer had to be so rude and wondered why he was trying to intimidate me.

And for a while, things were pretty uneventful. Then one day, when I was scheduled to work the graveyard shift, 11 PM to 7 AM, I went to the gym at noon, as usual, and had an especially hard training session. I got back with enough time to catch a nap before work, and my cousin Kathy agreed to wake me.

When she got distracted I overslept, and on awaking hurried out of the house to catch the bus to work. But when I arrived at the bus stop, the bus was pulling away. Not wanting to miss work, I decided to walk the ten city blocks.

I began walking and noticed a group of people standing on the corner in the distance, just in front of a small grocery store on the corner—just the kind of corner store that Philadelphia is so famous for. I also noticed a man stagger out of the corner store with a brown paper bag in his hand, and about that time I heard a dog bark in the distance. I picked up a branch that was lying at the side of the street, just in case the dog was loose and tried to attack.

Continuing to walk at a fast pace, I passed the man who had exited the store. As I passed the man, I heard him scream, "You've got to be a *bold* Nigger."

I couldn't tell if the man was speaking to me, or to himself, and so I ignored the comment and kept walking. Soon, I heard more screaming, as the man continued, "YOU! *I mean YOU!* You must be a bold Nigger. I ain't shot me a Nigger in a *long* time."

By this time, I knew that the man had to be speaking to me, so I continued to walk and glanced back at him.

This slight recognition must have fueled the old man, and he continued, "Yeah, you Nigger, I mean *you.*"

Next, I heard the sound of a paper bag rustling, and then what sounded like the hammer of a revolver. So when the man yelled, "STOP!" I froze in my tracks, waiting for the hammer to drop and questioning my judgment in trying to get to work in a neighborhood that I now knew was not safe.

The old man continued to yell, and as he got involved in his own words, he began to cry. Finally, as I was still standing, wondering what to do to try to calm the man, I heard the man shout, *"Get out, you fuckin' Nigger!* I don't *ever* want to see you in this neighborhood again!"

I resumed walking, and as I headed away from the man, I heard his final, "I don't mean walk, Nigger. I mean *RUN.*"

I didn't need to hear those words twice. I broke out in a fast jog, and continued all the way to work.

Arriving at work, my clothes wet with sweat, I cursed under my breath for being moved to rotating shift, and vowed that I would never again try to walk to work. Although for the most part I enjoyed the work, getting there just wasn't worth the danger that the city held. From now on, I promised myself, I would take the bus, which I felt was safe.

But the events in the city, combined with the difficulty arranging my training schedule, already had me wondering if it was time for a change.

"No one is born hating another person because of the color of his skin, or his background, or his religion. People must learn to hate, and if they can learn to hate, they can be taught to love, for love comes more naturally to the human heart than its opposite".
Nelson Mandela, Long Walk to Freedom

"No man can put a chain around the neck of his fellow man without at last finding the other end fastened about his own neck." -- Frederick Douglass
1883, Speech at Civil rights Mass Meeting, Washington, D.C.

"The limits of tyrants are prescribed by the endurance of those whom they oppose." -- Frederick Douglass

"We have enjoyed so much freedom for so long that we are perhaps in danger of forgetting how much blood it cost to establish the Bill of Rights."
Felix Frankfurter

"Liberty is always dangerous, but it is the safest thing we have." -- Harry Emerson Fosdick

"Liberty has never come from the government. Liberty
has always come from the subjects of it. This history of
liberty is a history of resistance."
Woodrow Wilson

"Freedom has its life in the hearts, the actions, the spirit of
men and so it must be daily earned and refreshed – else
like a flower cut from its life-giving roots, it will wither
and die." -- Dwight D. Eisenhower

"Those who deny freedom to others deserve it not for
themselves." -- Abraham Lincoln

"Nothing is the world is more dangerous than sincere
ignorance and conscientious stupidity."
Rev. Dr. Martin Luther King, Jr.
1963, Strength to Love

"And we who have toiled for freedom's law, have we
sought for freedom's soul? Have we learned at last that
human right is not a part but the whole?
John Boyle O'Reilly

"Give to every human being every right
that you claim for yourself." -- Robert Ingersoll

"We on this continent should never forget that men first
crossed the Atlantic not find soil for their ploughs but to
secure liberty for their souls." Robert J. McCracken

THE THIRD ROUND:

◆———————◆

MILITARY LIFE

Not long after that, while working the morning shift, I left work at 3 PM and went to the gym. Later that evening, I got off the subway one stop before Broad and Tasker, because I felt like walking home.

It was while walking home that I passed a Marine Corps recruiter's office, and after a moment of internal struggle, decided to take a minute and talk to the recruiter. After all, many fighters had been Marines. Among them were Ken Norton, Leon Spinks, and Gene Tunney.

I explained my goals to the recruiter, and mentioned that I was intrigued with Ken Norton, knowing that he was a former Marine and was now being trained by Eddie Futch. We also discussed Leon Spinks, who was also a former Marine and Olympic Gold Medalist, who now trained at Frazier's gym and was being managed by a big-time promoter, Butch Lewis. Then we talked about Sam Solomon, who used to train the great Sonny Liston.

Like every recruiter, this one did his job. He convinced me that like Ken Norton and Leon Spinks, I would be able to fight while in the Corps. We finished our conversation, and agreed to talk more the next day.

My mind was racing. I spoke to my sister and her husband. I also talked with my Uncle Rufus and Aunt Jenna about joining the Marine Corps. They all asked if that was really what I wanted to do and I assured them that it was.

I explained that the Marine Corps had a boxing team, and I also explained that when I spoke with Mama, she reminded me that my first boxing trainer was a Marine and if he could make it onto the boxing team, then so could I. I began thinking about what Mama would always say to me, "You can do whatever you want to, if you work at it."

On my way home the following day, I decided to take the test and later that day I took the physical, both of which I passed. I was placed onto delayed entry, and the next thing I knew, I was headed back home to Beaufort, South Carolina, to attend Parris Island Recruit Training.

Parris Island Recruit Training is famous for its unconventional methods of training their men and women. I had never seen anything like it.

There were officers and enlisted men who I thought were completely crazy. At first, I did not understand their methods and the threats they used. Although I tried to always do the right thing, I often felt I was at a disadvantage because in order to accomplish what I wanted to, I would have to follow orders, even if I didn't agree. There were times when the drill

"Most of us are blessed with
an amazing degree of physical sight.
It would truly be a shame if we use our ability
as an excuse for hatred." -- Zeke Wilson
September 2000, McCormick Federal Court

instructors would get in my face, threaten me, and look for a reaction. I learned not to show any reaction whatsoever.

Overall, recruit training was not as hard as everybody told me. I was in great physical shape. I got accustomed to the mental training and continued to work hard to make it out of recruit training and into the Marine Corps.

Because of my confidence and leadership skills, they assigned me a position as Platoon Guide. As such, I was responsible for four squad leaders, and ultimately, for each person in their squad. If a platoon member did not pass inspection, or didn't know their general orders, or fell out of step, it was my responsibility. I was responsible to make sure that recruit fell into step with the rest of his team.

Sometimes, my job included counseling recruits who were not making the transition into the Corps smoothly. Not everyone who attends recruit training becomes a Marine. Some don't have the physical stamina. Some don't have the mental acuity. Others begin to display symptoms of instability and are weeded out.

My Platoon began with eighty-nine recruits. At the end of training, there were "forty-seven highly motivated, truly dedicated, rough, tough, mean, green amphibious fighters" who made it through training and graduated as Marines. I had the proud privilege of standing with the remaining members of my Platoon as they took their place on the Parade Deck for graduation.

I was even more proud that Mama and a few of my sisters were able to make the trip to see me graduate and officially become a member of the United States Marine Corps.

I was assigned duty as a 2131, an artillery mechanic, and so after a brief leave I reported to Aberdeen Proving Grounds for artillery training. The facility at Aberdeen is an Army base that is used to instruct both Army and Marine troops assigned to artillery and tanks.

My job was to learn to repair and service the big guns that shoot from twelve to fifteen miles. I specialized in the Howitzer 05, the 55, the 9-inch, tanks and the M-track.

As an incentive, the training personnel offered choice of duty station to each man who scored first in their branch on the final exam. I scored second to an Army guy—but first in my class of Marines, and so was presented with my choice of duty stations.

There were many times in the military when it is best to keep your thoughts to yourself. This was one of them. I was being given the choice of duty stations. I already had conversations with one of the instructors at Aberdeen, Sergeant Birdsell, about Camp Pendleton and Camp Lejeune. Both had a boxing team. He said that Camp Pendleton was a better base. He also said that I would love Camp Pendleton, and if boxing was my goal, Pendleton is it.

I thought silently, "I just want to get to my duty station so I can apply for the Boxing Team." But what came out audibly was more like, "I'd like Camp Pendleton."

After all, I didn't join the Marine Corps to be an artillery mechanic; I joined the Corps so I could get onto the boxing team.

When I got to Camp Pendleton, Sergeant Birdsell was there on the base. My Master Gunnery Sgt., "Top" Likens, didn't like me to talk about boxing around the artillery base. In his opinion, "If the Marine Corps wanted you to be a boxer, it would have trained you to be a boxer. The Corps didn't make you a boxer; it made you an artillery mechanic. That's what you're being paid for, and that's what you're going to do."

I was well aware by this time that the Corps doesn't take recruits and train them to be boxers. You have to apply for placement on the team. But Top was a very strong-willed, hard-core Marine. He had been in active duty for thirty-three years, and had earned the highest rank you can attain as an enlisted man, a Master Gunnery Sergeant. I didn't want to buck the system. Plus, Top had a reputation for not taking anything from anyone, especially a mere Private First Class like me.

My first assignment was with Hotel Battery. My unit had four batteries. The other three batteries were Mike, Golf, and India. They had their own assigned gun docs—Sgt. Birdsell, Sgt. Parris, and Lance Corporal Acceras.

As in training, I did my best and excelled at my job. I went out into the field with Hotel Battery, and when the guns weren't firing properly I would test and repair them. Because I tried to be a motivation to all of the guys in the battery, I was well-liked and was promoted in rank to Lance Corporal while in the field with Hotel Battery.

"Top" Likens made sure of it; he felt I was a good field Marine. After a short time, he said, "I don't want to stand in the way of someone whose heart is into something." So he told me that if I wanted to apply for the boxing team, he would approve the application.

As soon as I received this "green light" from Top I made my application. It was due to the high recommendation of Master Gunnery Sgt. Top Likens that I was accepted to the USMC Boxing Team, and division cut me a set of orders. The Boxing Coach already heard about me from guys who had seen me box before, and so the Coach knew I would be a real asset to the team.

My dreams were finally coming true. I was able to train and receive a paycheck at the same time. The boxing team trained together and jogged together. Our training was consistent and challenging.

Although I sometimes missed my artillery unit at Los Pogos, I stayed and trained and traveled with the boxing team. While in the Corps, I had the opportunity to fight often and to build my boxing record to 147-3. I did exceptionally well, and made the All-Marine team. That provided opportunities for international competition, and I remained an amateur until I left the Corps with an Honorable Discharge, a Good Conduct Medal and a Meritorious Mass.

About one month before getting out of the USMC, I was sent back to the artillery unit at Twenty-Nine Palms, California, to await my discharge. Back on the base, I had become quite a celebrity with the artillery unit. One day a local writer came and interviewed me for an article in the Marine Corps Magazine, *"Leatherneck"*.

◆————————◆

Chuck Donaldson was a retired Marine Captain who owned a gas station in town. He told me, "I've read a lot about you, and am very impressed. I'm curious whether you'll be turning pro now that you've had an extensive amateur career. I have a friend in New York City, Joe Sirola, who could help arrange your pro debut."

I listened carefully to what Chuck had to say, and then asked, "So what are you saying, that you'd like to be my manager?"

Chuck replied, "That's what I'm saying." I didn't have a manager at the time, so I was interested.

About that time I also met a young nurse named Kimberly Glover and began to see her whenever I could find the time. Kim would later prove to be a very important part of my life.

After numerous phone calls, Chuck was able to arrange my debut at Madison Square Garden. As soon as the news of my debut circulated, the Marine Corps magazine, *"Leatherneck"*, wrote an article entitled, "Pugilist Bound for Madison Square Garden." Immediately, people from the community and the base were congratulating me constantly, and my celebrity status increased.

Chuck's friend Joe Sirola was a well-known actor. Sirola played the character Reno in Clint Eastwood's film "Hang 'Em High". He also appeared on the famous television show, "Gunsmoke", and his voice is well-known due to the numerous voice-overs that he has done for commercials on both radio and television.

Sirola was a good friend of John Condon, President of Madison Square Garden, and had the connections to

Hotline Sports

Pugilist bound for Madison Square Garden

"A friend of mine in New York, John Condon, President of Madison Square Garden, had the necessary connections in the world of boxing to get this fight, and in the very near future will be working directly with Wilson. The next thing I knew, I was on the phone with Joe Sirola, my business partner and well known actor and announcer. After verification of Wilson's record, we had the match. It will be a four rounder aired on local television .there. It's small, but it is a start," Donaldson concluded.

The night of Jan. 14, Cpl. Ezekeil Wilson will have some pretty heavy hitting and experienced past champions in the corner with him. Training Wilson in New York will be, Emile Griffith, a former welterweight and middleweight champion. Also attending the fight for a look at a possible "former Marine" boxing world great will be Rocky Graziano and Jake (Raging Bull) Lamotta, both former middleweight champions.

When asked to comment on his upcoming fight, Cpl. Wilson said, "I'm not Ali, so I'm not going to say what's going to happen and in what fashion. I will say that I do feel good and that the good Lord has blessed me. What else can I say, but whoever I get into the ring with had better be ready...cause I am." **SSgt. Brad Heck**

Cpl. Wilson runs through a routine as manager, Chuck Donaldson looks on. (Photo by SSgt. Brad Heck) arrange my pro debut there, at the venue legendary for top-level championship boxing. Sirola also arranged to have the former middle-weight champion Emile Griffith train me while I was in New York. Jake Lamotta and Rocky Graciano would also be in attendance.

I felt like I was on top of the world. I called all my friends in Philadelphia and South Carolina and gave them the great news. Some of my friends made it to the Garden to watch me fight. After one hundred fifty fights, I felt well-tuned and in great shape.

My sister Frenisee drove to New York to see me step into the ring for the first time as a pro fighter. My career was on track as I began an undefeated record.

It was an unforgettable night for so many reasons. The Marine Corps had refined my confidence, my sister had finally gotten to see me fight, I won my pro debut, and experienced the atmosphere at Madison Square Garden.

Having my debut at the Garden was a dream come true. A writer for the New York Post must have agreed, and wrote an article about the fight entitled "Fighter's Dream Comes True".

"Liberty means responsibility. That is why
most men dread it." -- George Bernard Shaw
1905, *Man and Superman*, "Maxims: Liberty and Equality"

"Freedom is the will to be responsible to ourselves."
Nietzsche, 1888, Twilight of the Idols

"The ultimate measure of a man is not where he stands in
moments of comfort and convenience, but where he
stands at times of challenge and controversy."
Rev. Dr. Martin Luther King, Jr.
1963, Strength to Love.

"No man is above the law and no man below it."
Theodore Roosevelt

"Our lives begin to end
the day we become silent
about things that matter."
Rev. Dr. Martin Luther King, Jr.

"It is often easier to become outraged by injustice half a
world away than by oppression and discrimination half a
block from home." -- Carl T. Rowan

"We must be free not because we claim freedom, but
because we practice it." -- William Faulkner

Boxer's dream starts at Forum

By LEONARD LEWIN

ZEKE WILSON, a heavyweight boxer fighting as a professional for the first time on Friday's Felt Forum card, sat and listened as Garden boxing president John Condon and matchmaker Harold Weston recalled how they never heard from Gerry Cooney on a $1-million offer to fight Renaldo Snipes.

Zeke had heard about those kind of numbers and, in fact, that's why he's decided on a boxing career after a Marine stint that ended only last Thursday. But he never had been in the same room with $1 million before — even though it was only conversation — and now he was even more determined to win when he starts fighting for money Friday.

"I've got a long way to go," the 23-year-old, 227-pounder from Philadelphia, who intends to fight out of New York, said. He's the biggest unknown on an 11-bout show that will feature unbeaten Eddie Gregg (12-0-1 with 12 KOs), junior middleweight Mark Medal (15-1 with 13 KOs) and welterweight Pedro Vilella (10-0-1 with 4 KOs) in 10-rounders.

Wilson goes in a four-rounder against 20-year-old Guy Ramey of Lima, O., who also will be making his pro debut. It figures to be a slasher because each has been through the amateur wars. Wilson was 147-3 and the AAU champ in 1979 while Ramey was 47-9.

Meanwhile, Gregg vs Barry (The Fighting Postman) Funches promises to be the best fight of the night. Gregg, a 6-4, 220-pound former football player at Winston-Salem, and Funches, a 33-year-old who carries the mail on 52d St. and Fifth Ave., used to spar against one another.

Now it's for real.

- 71 -

"The sound of tireless voices is the price we pay for the
right to hear the music of our own opinions."
Adlai Stevenson
Speech, New York City, August 28, 1952

"I believe that unarmed truth and unconditional love will
have the final word in reality. This is why right,
temporarily defeated, is stronger than evil triumphant."
Rev. Dr. Martin Luther King, Jr.

"I am the inferior of any man whose rights I trample
underfoot." -- Horace Greeley

"He that would make his own liberty secure,
must guard even his enemy from opposition;
for if he violates this duty
he establishes a precedent that will reach himself."
Thomas Paine

"For to be free is not merely to cast off one's chains, but
to live in a way that respects and enhances the freedom of
others." -- Nelson Mandela

Alfonzo Inzarry-El

EN FELT FORUM VIERNES. El Felt Forum del Madison Square Garden presenta este viernes su primer programa del nuevo año con los estelaristas Mark Medal, de Puerto Rico y Chris Linson, de Nuevo México. En la foto, de izquierda, otros participantes como Eddie Gregg, El Cartero Barry boricua Pedro Vilella y Zeke Wilson, de San Diego, California.

NEW YORK POST

"Human rights are not a privilege conferred by government. They are every human being's entitlement by virtue of his humanity. The Right to life does not depend, and must not be contingent, on the pleasure of anyone else." -- Mother Teresa

"The good neighbor looks beyond the external accidents and discerns those inner qualities that make all men human and, therefore, brothers."
Rev. Dr. Martin Luther King, Jr.

"Of all the so-called natural human rights that have ever been invented, liberty is least likely to be cheap and is never free of cost." – Robert Heinlein

"It may be true that the law cannot make a man love me, but it can stop him from lynching me, and I think that's pretty important."
Rev. Dr. Martin Luther King, Jr.

"The whole of the Bill (of Rights) is a declaration of the right of the people at large or considered as individuals…It establishes some rights of the individual as unalienable and which consequently, no majority has a right to deprive them of." -- Albert Gallatin

THE FOURTH ROUND:

◆———————◆

PRO CAREER

On my journey in the world of boxing, I learned a lot about boxing and many legendary people who made boxing what it is today. I wanted to emulate as many of them as I could as my career took me from San Diego to Los Angeles. Kim went to Los Angeles with me, always providing moral support and helping to keep me focused.

I continued to live on the West Cost with Kim and the following year, we had a baby boy named Marcus. I was so happy that I had a son I could watch grow up and teach some of the things I was doing. In the afternoons after training, I would return home from the gym and Marcus would be jumping and laughing. We would play together on the floor.

It was a great focus after having serious career conversations, and was relaxing. I often thought that boxing was rough and didn't want my son to become a prizefighter, because I was struggling to do it myself.

When I did pushups, Marcus would try to do them with me. Marcus helped to give me a purpose. I discussed my future in boxing with Kim, and how we could take it to a different level.

I enjoyed living in Los Angeles, and soon I had a training schedule that provided the balance I needed. I did my roadwork at 4 AM, then returned home to shadowbox and hit the heavy bag and speed bag in the morning. Then in the afternoon, I would go to the gym. I'd return from the gym and do pushups and sit-ups to strengthen my upper body. It became habit and everything was on track.

One day, while working out at Main Street Gym, a gentleman named Robert Baran began a conversation with me. Mr. Baran said he heard about my fight in Madison Square Garden, and that I did a very good job. We continued our conversation after my training session was over. As it turned out, he was a big boxing fan and he invited me to his home in Beverly Hills, California, for a boxing party attended by many boxing celebrities. It was a lot of fun, and during the party we watched the Ray Mancini versus Art Frias World Championship fight.

At the gym there were a lot of heavyweight boxers, so sparring was good. One day, the guys were talking about Muhammad Ali's gym in Santa Monica, California, saying how nice it was, so I had to check it out. While there, I met a man named Norman Henry, who was actively involved in professional boxing. He knew George Foreman well, and was a very good friend of the World Heavyweight Champion Larry Holmes.

We spoke about fighters and his involvement with them. Norman was able to teach me things about boxing outside of the ring.

The next day I returned to Ali's gym, and ran into a good friend from Philadelphia, Charles Singleton. We talked about the old days, and he returned with me to my house where he met Kim and Marcus. It was like old times, and it reminded me how far I had come.

Later, Norman invited us to his home, where we had a long conversation about developments in the sport. I was thrilled at the news that Larry Holmes was coming to Los Angeles to work with Lee Majors on his show "The Fall Guy", and would be training in Santa Monica at Muhammad Ali's gym.

I recounted that when I first got to Philadelphia, I wanted so badly to work with guys like that. At the time, Norman's wife was making sandwiches while we sat in the living room, just off of the kitchen. Charles agreed that it would be unreal, a dream come true, to work with the Heavyweight Champion of the World. We both agreed that would be sparring at its best.

Norman was carrying a tray of sandwiches into the room and rejoined the conversation, saying, "It can take years for something like that to happen."

So, I didn't think too much more about the conversation at the time, because an opportunity like that was out of my reach. At the time, Larry Holmes was the world champion and had sparring partners who were very well qualified. So, Larry was in good hands.

However, Norman's wife prompted Norman to contact Larry Holmes' training camp and recommend me as a sparring partner because, although I was new as a pro, she felt that my skills and attitude were sufficient to give me a chance.

One afternoon the phone rang. The call was from Norman. We began talking, and his tone got serious. "Zeke," he said, "There's a pre-paid ticket for you on United Airlines to go to Pennsylvania."

"For what?" I asked.

Norman continued, "To work as a sparring partner with Larry Holmes."

"Yeah, right." I couldn't believe it, and insisted that Norman was playing some sort of game with me.

Norman quickly replied, "Call the airline, and call me back."

Looking at me, Kim saw the expression on my face, and asked me what the call was about.

I told her, and she smiled. Curious, I picked up the phone, not really believing the airline would confirm Norman's news. But the terminal operator at LAX confirmed there was a prepaid ticket for Zeke Wilson to ABE Airport, paid by Larry Holmes Enterprises.

I had to sit down, still holding the phone. Kim was shouting for joy. Marcus didn't understand the excitement, but joined in, dancing around and screaming.

Once again, my dream to become a sparring partner for the world's best heavyweight champions had come true. I called Norman, who laughed and said, "Zeke, you should watch what you wish for."

All of this happened within a seventy-two-hour period, and I had only one week to board the plane to go to Holmes' camp.

That's when the reality of the situation set in-- realization that this was a huge step in my career. I had never worked with anyone like Larry Holmes. I was so excited about going to Easton, Pennsylvania, that I didn't sleep for days, knowing that as a sparring partner, if you don't work hard, you won't be there long. I also reminded myself that I had boxed with Joe Frazier, the former heavyweight champ of the world, the first man to beat Muhammad Ali; also, with Jimmy Young and Ron Lyles, who fought with George Foreman, knocking him down--telling myself all the way on the plane that Larry Holmes wouldn't do any more to me than those guys did, that Larry Holmes was just a man, and that if Larry could hit me, I could also hit him.

When I got to Easton, the atmosphere of being in camp with the heavyweight champ was more than most people would ever dream of. At that time people were there that I had not seen since the amateurs--Jerry Williams and Marvin Stinson.

That relaxed me a little bit, but then I started hearing horror stories from the sparring partners and the staff. They showed me a corn field, and said, "You know, Larry buried his last sparring partner in that field."

All of the guys looked at me and laughed. Although I was happy and grateful, I was not afraid. Anyway, I began to tell people that I was in camp with the champ.

I stayed with Larry Holmes during the years when

Sparring Partner Zeke Wilson
At the Holmes v. Bey fight
1985, Las Vegas, Nevada

Larry was the best fighter in the world. Working with Larry gave me the experience of truly training with the best.

During my time with him, I met other people who had an impact on my career and my life. One day, while training with the champ at the Riviera Hotel in Las Vegas, the training session was open to the public. In the audience there were a large number of celebrities. Among them were Grammy Award Winner Lou Rawls, Robert Guillaume, who was starring in the title role of television's Emmy award-winning show "Benson", and America's Singing Poet, Steve DePass.

After the training session was over, I found myself shaking hands with a lot of the celebrities in attendance. Steve DePass and Robert Guillaume expressed how easy I made the sparring session look. Both were performing in Las Vegas at the time, Steve DePass at the Tropicana Hotel and Robert Guillaume at the Riviera.

I attended both of their shows. The first night was at the Riviera, and Robert performed sensationally. He was headlined by the Solid Gold Dancers. I sat in the front row while he was performing. He had the lighting

If Holmes' prediction is accurate, he'll earn $1 million per round in his fight with Coetzee, whose share of the purse will be about $3.5 million ...

Holmes' workouts at his Canal Street training center are open to the public and will continue through the first week of May. Sessions begin at 5 p.m. Mondays, Tuesdays, Thursdays and Fridays, and at 3 p.m. on Saturdays. Sundays and Wednesdays are his off days. Sparring partners in camp include Jerry Williams, Rufus Hadley, Zeke Wilson and Phil Brown. James Broad, a member of the 1980 U.S. Olympic team who's off to a good start in his pro career, is also training at Holmes' gym ...

● ● ●

Since Holmes gave up his WBC title, that organization has dropped him from its rankings altogether. The WBC's current ratings have Greg Page, Michael Dokes, Mike Weaver, Pinklon Thomas, Trevor Berbick, David Bey. Jeff Sims, Lucien Rodriquez, Frank Bruno and Renaldo Snipes in line behind champion Tim Witherspoon. Holmes has beaten five fighters in that group, including Witherspoon, and a couple of others in the WBC's Top 10 have yet to even face a first-rate opponent ... But if you think the WBC ratings are ludicrous, consider this: Although Holmes is unbeaten in 45 pro bouts crew shine the spotlight on me, and announced, "Ladies and Gentlemen, the next heavyweight Champion, Zeke Wilson."

He continued by saying that he attended the training session and watched the World Heavyweight Champion, Larry Holmes, box with me, and it was a great performance. At that time, the entire audience clapped as I stood and raised both hands. It was a memorable night.

The second night was highlighted by Steve DePass performing at the Tropicana Hotel and Casino. His show was equally good. I had a front-row seat and was very much impressed. I had come to Las Vegas and was able to watch two entertainers who were champions in their own arena.

A few weeks later, Larry defeated James "Bonecrusher" Smith. Afterwards, I found myself leaving Las Vegas en route to Manhattan, New York to meet Robert Guillaume at Gallagher's Steak House for a meeting arranged by Steve DePass to discuss a managerial contract. A few days later, Robert and I entered into a managerial contract, and Steve became my advisor. Steve and Robert contracted Don Elbaum as my promoter.

When I called back home to give Kim the good news, she told me that she was very happy for me, but that we needed to talk about our future. I caught a flight back to Los Angeles and tried to convince her that everything would be okay. But she had already made different plans.

So, we sat and talked about a future apart. I remember leaving Los Angeles, thinking, "Did my boxing career get between us?"

I continued to train with Larry Holmes, and a few months later I fought for the second time at Madison Square Garden, on the undercard of the Leon Spinks versus Kip Kane championship bout.

My time with Larry also opened my eyes to the business side of boxing. Larry was under contract with famous promoter Don King, who although at times controversial, was and is the best in the business.

I finally ended my amateur career with a record of 147-3, and my undefeated pro career with a record of 17-0-1.

FRIDAY THE **13**TH

OF DECEMBER 1985
FIRST BOUT 7:30 P.M.

WBC CONTINENTAL OF AMERICAS
HEAVYWEIGHT CHAMPIONSHIP

12 ROUNDS

SPINKS JINX VS. **THE LUCK OF THE IRISH**

GUADAGNO & PALARDY
PROMOTERS

DON ELBAUM
MATCHMAKER

FORMER HEAVYWEIGHT CHAMPION   "IRISH"

LEON SPINKS   KIP KANE

10 ROUND SEMI FINAL — JR. LIGHTWEIGHTS

JOHNNY DE LAROSA VS. **AL MARTINO**
DOMINICAN REPUBLIC   WASHINGTON, D.C.

ALSO IN ACTION

JR. MIDDLEWEIGHT - LEVITTOWN, N.Y.
MIKE CARBONE

JR. MIDDLEWEIGHT - BUTLER, N.J.
JOHN "The Irish Cannonball" **KINNEY**

LIGHT HEAVYWEIGHT - BROOKLYN, N.Y.
CARMINE VENEZIANO

MIDDLEWEIGHT - PORT CHESTER, N.Y.
LYLE WILLIAMS

NEW YORK WELTERWEIGHT
MIKE TRICARICO

T.V.'s "BENSON'S" UNDEFEATED HEAVYWEIGHT SENSATION
ZEKE WILSON

$30.00 RINGSIDE
$15.00 RESERVED

SPECIAL ADDED ATTRACTION

ISRAEL'S NEWEST STAR
SCHLOMO NIAZOV

TICKETS ARE ON SALE AT ALL TICKETRON
OUTLETS AND MADISON SQUARE GARDEN
ALSO: MAQUIRE'S CAFE - 800 2nd AVE. BET. 42nd & 43rd STS., NYC - (212) 370-5454
VALLEY TRANSPORTATION - 582 VALLEY ROAD, WEST ORANGE, N.J. - (201) 676-8066

the felt forum

MADISON SQUARE GARDEN CENTER - 8th AVE. BET. 31st & 33rd STS.

◆————————◆

By observing and learning the business end of the sport from the best, I was preparing to step into the next phase of my career in boxing. Watching Don King closely, I admired his accomplishments in the business of boxing.

I had learned a lot from the sport, having watched Don King as a promoter, Lou Duva as a manager and Eddie Futch as a trainer—very successful people, and said to myself, "If they can do it, so can I."

So I wanted to become a successful trainer, manager, and promoter. That would enable me to continue my career far beyond the bounds of the ring ropes.

Eager to begin, I placed an ad in the newspaper to find fighters who were interested in turning professional. Out of the numerous responses I received, one was a phone call from a fighter named Luis Melendez, who I began to train.

My mind raced back to my amateur days, working with Macauley Washburn. It felt good. I began training Luis and about that time other fighters responded to the newspaper ad.

All of the fighters were training at the YMCA in Allentown, Pennsylvania. I was training ten kids between the ages of nine through twenty-three. That was a lot of fighters for me to handle, but I loved it.

My training schedule was from 3 PM to 8 PM five days a week. I trained my fighters at the YMCA for about a year before finding a location for a gym on the east side of the city and had it ready to open within two weeks.

By that time, I was training about twelve fighters. They were making steady progress, and were getting to a point in their training where they would soon be ready for their amateur debut.

I worked on their skills and had them each fight a few amateur bouts. At that point, I formed Wilson Promotional Group so that I could properly manage their progress and arrange good opportunities for them through well-matched competition.

In the summer of 1989, I promoted my first amateur event at the Airport Bingo Hall in Allentown, Pennsylvania. I was very excited that people came from all over the city to attend. Having little help, I worked twice as hard to make it a great night.

Posters were made and distributed, there were ads placed on radio and TV, I found a few local sponsors and sold ads in the program book.

Much of the procedure came easily, because Bob Arum and Don King were the biggest promoters in the sport, and I was able to copy their success. In the meantime, I was still training fighters five days a week. The night of the fight, there were eight bouts. The kids put on their best performance. Everyone in attendance was very pleased.

Needless to say, my early success reinforced my plan to train, manage and promote the sport that had been my career. Like a retired baseball player may go on to become a baseball manager, or a retired football player may become a football coach, I had already made the step into my future career.

All of the fighters in the gym were working very hard to be the best, but Luis worked above them all. In 1990, I successfully negotiated for Luis Melendez to fight on the undercard of the WBO Light Heavyweight

Championship bout between Michael Moorer and Mario Melo, and the WBO Super Middleweight Championship bout between Tommy Hearns and Michael Olajide, a Top Rank show held at the Taj Mahal Casino in Atlantic City and aired on Showtime TV.

It was a great night of boxing. Tommy Hearns defeated Michael Olajide. My fighter, Luis Melendez, lost a very close split decision to Frank Toledo. Toledo later went on to become the Bantamweight Champion of the World. I felt that Luis did his best that night, but he came up short.

◆——————◆

My mind raced back to my Marine Corps days and I decided to stage a fight between the All-Army team out of Fort Bragg, North Carolina, and the All-Navy team out of Norfolk, Virginia.

Being a former Marine Corps boxer, I knew what I was doing when I arranged an amateur fight card that matched service teams. The Army versus Navy— something like that can heat up a gym faster than you can say, "Look out, here come the Marines!" But, I was bent on trying to bring boxing into the Lehigh Valley.

The Army coach was from Philadelphia. He also trained at Joe Frazier's gym, and hung out at the All-Star Gym on Sixth and Snyder in South Philadelphia.

After listening to both coaches, I became convinced that it was going to be a great show. Believe me, it was a "war" from start to finish.

I was able to arrange a hotel host to provide rooms, and booked a much larger facility. The Ag Hall at the Allentown Fairgrounds was three times the size of the Airport Bingo Hall, and was perfect for the event.

Early in '91, we were able to host a boxing team from Leningrad, Soviet Union. The team consisted of nineteen boxers, two coaches, and one interpreter. I arranged their flight and a two-week tour during which they trained in the United States. They also signed autographs and held public training and sparring sessions for the American people.

Their interpreter, Natasha, explained that the boxers represent the Army boxing club. They train three times a day—morning, afternoon, and evening.

Boxing Exhibition Gives Fans Chance To See Soviet Fighters

By MIKE CUMMINGS
Staff Writer

The Russians are coming to Savannah.

And they're doing so to help a good cause.

The CAC Sports Army Club, from Leningrad, U.S.S.R. will be participating in a boxing exhibition with the Mid-Atlantic Boxing Club Nov. 30 at the Savannah Civic Center. Former Miami Dolphin star Mercury Morris will make a guest appearance at the exhibition.

All 12 Olympic boxing weight classifications will be fought at the exhibition.

"The fighters have won all types of titles," fight promoter Zeke Wilson said of the Soviets. "They are Olympic hopefuls."

On the other side, the Mid-Atlantic Boxing Club is comprised of Olympic hopefuls from the East. According to Wilson, several fighters that will appear in Savannah are Golden Gloves and amateur champions.

Wilson, from Northhampton, Pa., a suburb of Philadelphia, was a former sparring partner of former world heavyweight champion Larry Holmes for six years before turning his talents to promoting fights. He, working from his promotional company, Best Of The Best Promotions, have promoted six shows in his career.

Part of the proceeds of the fight will go to help drug education services in the Chatham County area. According to Pat Leslie, the administrative coordinator of health and physical education for the Savannah-Chatham County public school system, Wilson has agreed to funnel 25 percent of the proceeds of the exhibitions to help with drug education in the area.

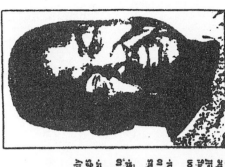

WILSON: Fight promoter

"The money will go primarily into a fund so that we can buy things that we can't buy through our federal grants,'" Leslie said.

Some of the money will also go to help the DARE (Drug Abuse Resistance Education) program.

Wilson said he decided to try his hand at bringing the exhibitions to Savannah after beginning his fighting career in the area.

"I fought here before,'' Wilson said. "But, Savannah then was a big fight town. I always said to myself that I'm going to come back to the place that I really truly got started. This is the first place I ever put on gloves and got started, right here in the Savannah area.

"Along the way, I went on to become the sparring partner for Larry Holmes. But, along with that, I never forgot where I got started and I got started, right here in Savannah.''

After Savannah, the Russians will participating in an exhibition in Charleston, S.C. on Dec. 7.

Wilson said he is also hopeful of bringing a Cuban national boxing team into Savannah for an exhibition.

She also explained that there is a lot of pressure on athletes in Moscow. When Natasha finished with the fighters' backgrounds, the audience began to ask questions about life in the Soviet Union.

I learned that most event promotions run smoothly, and that some produced big headaches, but it was clear after a while that training and event promotions were things I could excel at comfortably in this phase of my career.

After learning to run amateur events, I began running pro events. My first was at the Sheraton Station Square Hotel in Pittsburgh in November, 1992. The first order of business was to obtain a promoter's license through the Pennsylvania Boxing Commission. I applied, paid the license fee and the event bond, and began to make arrangements for my event.

After negotiating contracts with the hotel, I began contracting fighters, and started advertising and marketing my event.

I put my best foot forward and started working with the hotel staff. Both the President and Vice President of the hotel were very pleased with the way

**GREATER PITTSBURGH FANS
YOU'VE SEEN THE REST
NOW WATCH THE BEST!**

WILSON PROMOTIONAL GROUP

**PRESENTS LIVE
WED. NOV. 25
PROFESSIONAL BOXING**

from the Sheraton Station Square Hotel

MAIN EVENT

Pittsburgh Undefeated Jr. Welterweight Sensation

RALPH "TIGER" JONES –vs.– REGGIE STRICKLAND

West Virginia Heavyweight Champ

WEST TURNER –vs.– CURTIS GIBSON

Undefeated Heavyweight Knockout Artist

GARY "BULL" WINMAN –vs.– ANDRE CROWER

Also in Action

Former U.S. Marine

DEMETRIUS "MIGHTY MEECH" JENNING –vs.– TONY WEST

ROBERT "THE HITMAN" BRIGGS –vs.– CLEARANCE WILLIAMS

BEANARD WRIGHT –vs.– GERMAIN DUNLOW

and MICHAEL GARROW

Special Guest Appearance
Former Two Time World Heavyweight Champ

"TERRIBLE" TIM WITHERSPOON

LOCATION:
Sheraton Station Square Hotel
7 Station Square Drive
Pittsburgh, PA

Doors Open – 6:30 PM

TICKETS AVAILABLE
**At the
door or at**
Jimmy's Post Tavern
Tel: 562-0238

TICKET PRICE:
Golden Ring Side $28.50
Ring Side $23.50
Gen. Admission $18.50

Fights Start – 8:00 PM

the promotion was going. I was working very hard, trying not to make any mistakes.

The event was a night of excitement. The crowd enjoyed the seven bouts that featured unbeaten Ralph "Tiger" Jones. When Ralph Jones defeated Reggie Strickland, the hotel's Vice President jumped from his ringside seat, clapping and cheering on the winner.

He then said, "My staff and I have worked with local boxing promoters in the past." He continued by saying, "Our hotel has the reputation of being a site for top-level boxing entertainment. Because we found in Zeke honesty and integrity, my staff and I committed ourselves to work with him to ensure a most successful event…Zeke never let us down. Through his diligence and professionalism, he had a crowd of over five hundred enthusiastic boxing fans in our Grand Ballroom. A well-organized event highlighted by a card full of talent. What an exciting night!"

I learned that night that there is really no difference between running amateur and pro events. The budget is higher, because professional boxers receive a monetary purse, but otherwise there is little difference.

At Sheraton

Jones Headlines Fight Card

By EDDIE JEFFERIES
Courier Sports Editor

Although he has spent most of his boxing life in and around the Philadelphia area, Zeke Wilson is well aware of Pittsburgh's former reputation as one of boxing's foremost meccas.

To that end, Wilson, an ex-boxer-turned-promoter, is doing his level best to resurrect the city's reputation in the way he knows best: by scheduling action-packed, competitive matchups in local venues. His initial effort locally will take place Wednesday, Nov. 25 at the Sheraton, Station Square, beginning at 8 pm.

Headlining the seven-bout card will be Ralph (Tiger) Jones, the undefeated jr. welterweight (140 pounds) sensation who, in the opinion of many observers, has an opportunity to make an impact on a national scale. He will be squaring off in the main event against Ohio's Reggie Strickland, who has vowed to end Jones' mercurial rise.

In exciting co-features, West Virginia Heavyweight Champion West Turner, a former Mountaineer gridder, is expected to trade heavy leather with Curtis Gibson, while knockout sensation Gary (Bull) Winman hopes to continue his KO streak against Andre Crower.

Other exciting matchups on the undercard will feature Demetrius (Mighty Meech) Jenning versus Tony West; Robert (Hit Man) Briggs against Clarence Williams; Bernard Wright against Germain Dunlow; and Michael Garrow against an as-yet unnamed opponent.

As a special added attraction, former two-time heavyweight champ "Terrible" Time Witherspoon will make a special guest appearance at ringside. A portion of the evening's proceeds will be donated to the Wood Street Commons, a shelter for the homeless.

Wilson, an ex-Marine boxing champion, had 144 amateur bouts and 17 pro matches before deciding that it was a lot more self-preserving to promote fights than engage in them. Afterall, he served as a sparring partner for a veritable "who's who" in boxing circles, among them the likes of Joe Frazier, Leon Spinks, Ron Lyle, Duane Bobick, James Broad, Jimmy Young, Jerry (The Bull) Martin, Randall (Tex) Cobb.

But his greatest claim to fame was and is his association with former heavyweight champ Larry Holmes. Appearing recently on the "Champions Sports Show," Wilson was asked how he survived what most assuredly must have been a host of ring wars.

"By keeping my hands up high and my eyes on my opponent," he said. "I enjoyed boxing. Joe (Frazier) taught me a lot, all those guys I sparred with, they also taught me a lot.

"But the guy who taught me the most was Larry Holmes. I worked with Larry for better than five and a half years. He was a great champion. I learned a lot and did a lot but I have a lot more to do. It's more like you came a long way, but you got a long way to go."

Perhaps his greatest learning experience was that a tireless worker can make as much outside the ring as he can make inside the square circle, with a lot less pain involved. Hence his transition from boxer to promoter. And like most who have observed Jones, the headliner on his upcoming card, Wilson is excited about the possibilities he sees in the up-and-coming prospect. "He (Jones) can be a world champion," Wilson admitted.

"When you want the best, you've got to get the best, and right now these fighters, Jones, Turner and Winman, are the best that Pittsburgh has to offer," said Wilson. And the Wilson Promotional Group, Inc. is dedicated to giving Pittsburgh the best... beginning Wednesday, Nov. 25.

Still, I was convinced that with a system and proper staffing I would be able to train a large number of fighters and run events monthly in major metropolitan areas throughout the United States, and began formatting a plan to do so.

I also knew that in order to fund such a large undertaking would require a focused plan and the background information to convince business men and women, who may not be familiar with the sport, of the feasibility of such a unique approach.

It took months to produce written documentation to support the financial projections and assemble displays. I spent a lot of time in the Allentown Library putting together background information and research to prepare the documents.

It was getting late one afternoon when a young lady walked in and asked me, "Is this seat taken?"

I replied, "No, it isn't. So, how are you? My name is Zeke."

Shaking my hand, she said, "I'm doing well. I'm Connie."

From that chance meeting, and over the course of

the next months and years, Connie would become my helper, my partner, and my wife.

Meanwhile, I continued to train and manage fighters. Connie and I bought a few income properties. We were married and were excited to find that we were expecting. Life seemed to be moving at warp speed.

We welcomed the birth of our daughter, who we named Florence after my mother.

Our research and documentation continued, and I was able to refine the business plan over the course of the next two years with the help of attorneys, accountants, and business professionals.

We worked together to finish the work I had started, and we even built a model of the proposed training facilities.

All of this work paid off when a local bank agreed to finance the cash we would need to set up our first promotional office. After reviewing several cities in the eastern part of the United States, I chose Boston as the first location for a promotional office.

Boston has a rich history in the sport of boxing.

History has it that John L. Sullivan was the first Heavyweight Champion of the World and he was from Boston. Boston is a city that produces a lot of boxing entertainment.

So, I called the Massachusetts Boxing Commission to request a Promoter's license, just as I did in Pennsylvania. The Commission sent me an application form, and I completed and returned it immediately.

A few weeks later, I received a letter from the panel of three Commissioners requesting me to submit a surety bond of ten thousand dollars in order to process my license request. I obtained the bond and returned it to the Commission, and it was time to begin promoting my event.

We found and leased office space in Woburn, Massachusetts, just north of the city, and I began advertising for marketing assistants. We hired a staff of local men and women to work in my office and assist me with the event promotion.

We found a venue and set a date to hold the event. The first event was planned for November 1, 1996, at Madison Park Community Center.

With any event, there are a myriad of details to attend to. The Governor Bradford Motel in Plymouth became the event sponsor. We made an agreement with the Greater Boston division of the Make-A-Wish Foundation to present a check for 20% of my event's proceeds during the event to benefit local kids with life-threatening illnesses.

Contracts were signed with a local ambulance and EMT service to be present for the event, and my office staff sold dozens of ads to appear in the program book distributed to those in attendance the night of the fight.

I assembled a fight card of eight bouts, including a number of fighters who would be coming in from Ohio. I knew that the local crowd would be interested in seeing a group of out-of-town fighters, and I could market and promote the excitement of the unknown talent.

I called Boxing Commissioner Stan Cooper, as I'd been instructed to do, to obtain bout approval. However, Cooper told me that all fighters would need to obtain mandatory HIV testing, which I wouldn't have time to get, as Cooper explained, because I had to complete the fight card at least ten days before my event. Therefore, the Commissioner explained, my event would have to be cancelled.

I was stunned. In spite of meeting with the Commissioners only a few months before and discussing plans for my first event, I had never heard of either requirement.

First, I appealed to Cooper to be reasonable, then informed him that I would have the event with him or without him. Cooper got very angry and replied, "Oh, no you won't! If you attempt to hold that event, I'll call the State Police and have your location shut down."

I hung up the phone, took a deep breath and called the Commission chairman, Kevin Brown. I explained to him the difficulty that I was having with Cooper. Brown assured me that he would have a talk with him, and that he'd get back with me.

The next time that I heard from Brown, he told me that my event was cancelled for not having enough bouts. He said, "You are now beyond the deadline that requires all fights to be submitted ten days before the event, and so the Commission is officially canceling the event."

"I believe there are more instances of the abridgment of
the freedom of the people by gradual and silent
encroachments of those in power than by violent and
sudden usurpations." -- James Madison
1788, Speech at Virginia Convention

"I am not interested in picking up crumbs of compassion
thrown from the table of someone who considers himself
my master. I want the full menu of rights."
Bishop Desmond Tutu
Quoted in *You Said a Mouthful*, by Ronald D. Fuchs

"The 'strength' of the people becomes weak
when we don't 'exercise' our rights."
Eric Schaub

"The constitution does not provide
for first and second class citizens."
Wendell L. Wilkie

"The highest patriotism is not a blind acceptance of
official policy, but a love of one's country deep enough to
call her to a higher standard."
George McGovern

"At the foundation of our civil liberties lies the principle that denies to government officials an exceptional position before the law and which subjects them to the same rules of conduct that are commands to the citizen."
Justice Louis D. Brandeis

"Freedom is that instant between when someone tells you to do something and when you decide how to respond."
Jeffrey Borenstein

"Let us forget such words, and all they mean, as Hatred, Bitterness and Rancor, Greed, Intolerance, Bigotry. Let us renew our faith and pledge to Man, his right to be Himself, and free." --Edna St. Vincent Millay

"We cannot defend liberty abroad by deserting it at home." -- Edward R. Murrow

"If you want to be free, there is but one way; it is to guarantee an equally full measure of liberty to all your neighbors. There is no other."
Carl Schurz

THE FIFTH ROUND:

◆———————◆

THE FIGHT BEGINS

Early the next morning, I drove into Boston for a visit to the office of the Boxing Commission. I also planned to get a copy of the Commission's regulations from the secretary.

When I walked into the office, the secretary greeted me. I introduced myself, and asked her for a copy of the current rules and regulations. She replied that she was instructed not to give me anything, and that besides they were being revised.

Another voice came from the other side of the room, saying, "If they're being changed, you have to give him a copy of the old ones."

Needless to say, I was more than just a little upset when the secretary repeated herself by saying, "I have instructions not to give him anything, and those are my instructions."

The Commission had cancelled my event for a reason that no one had ever heard of, and I needed some type of explanation for my event sponsors. The actions of the Commissioners had put me in a very uncomfortable situation.

Still, she refused to let me see a copy of the regulations, so I returned to the Governor Bradford Motel, very upset, and called an attorney for some advice. The attorney advised me that there are state regulations that could be obtained from either a law library or perhaps even a local public library.

So, we visited the public library at Plymouth,

Massachusetts, and found the staff to be very friendly and helpful. The librarian assisted us in finding the Code of Massachusetts Regulations, and we copied the entire section that dealt with the Boxing Commission.

I also called the Secretary of State's office, as the librarian had recommended, and spoke with Troy McHenry, who assured me that the 1993 revision was indeed the most recent and currently enforceable. He informed me that there was a revision that would come into effect in December of '96, but it was not in effect yet. His office made arrangements for me to purchase a copy from him.

I returned to the Governor Bradford to study the Regulations and to regroup. What I read in the Code of Massachusetts Regulations, or CMR, made me angry but very determined. It turned out that there was no ten-day rule in effect for submitting fighters on a fight card. In fact, the regulations gave the promoter up to seventy-two hours before the event for submitting fighters to the fight card.

And I also learned that the Commission was required by law to publish and distribute the current regulations to anyone who requested them.

Furthermore, the statutory amount of the bond was to be five thousand dollars—not the ten thousand dollars that they required of me.

Most importantly, there was no HIV testing requirement in the regulations at all.

Not one bit calmer, I called and demanded a meeting with the Chairman, to get an explanation for cancellation of my event. Armed with the CMRs, I spoke with Brown. He said, "I will see you at the meeting of the Promoters."

I felt he could not offer a reasonable explanation, and I made sure that the Chairman was aware of the expense involved and the loss they caused me.

Because the Governor appointed the Commissioners, I called the Governor's office and spoke with Joe Karshner, the Governor's aide. After supplying him with a written complaint, he said he'd see what he could do.

There was a Commission meeting for all licensed Promoters scheduled a week later, and I attended the meeting. When I walked in, Chairman Brown immediately came up to me and said, "I don't know what's wrong with you, coming to the State Building and causing a ruckus. We don't do that here. You've violated every rule and policy of the Commission…"

"Chairman Brown," I interrupted.

He continued, "I wanted to give you this after the meeting, but I might as well give it to you now."

He handed me a letter. I opened it and began reading. The letter began, "Loud shouting is no way to do business."

I stopped reading, and said to Brown, "If you assholes want loud shouting, I'll give you loud shouting. What the hell are you guys trying to do to me? You stopped my show one week ahead because of some dumbass ten-day rule!"

Brown screamed, "Calm down, man! Everybody has to follow the same rules."

I said, "That's bullshit! I got a copy of the State Regulations, and there is no ten-day rule in it."

Brown replied, "Zeke, the ten-day rule is our policy. What we need to do…"

I interrupted him, saying, "I'll tell you what you need to do—instead of writing letters telling me how to act, you need to reschedule my event."

Quietly, Brown replied, "Okay, man, we'll talk in my office after the meeting. We can resolve this then."

I added, "The only way we can resolve this is to reschedule my event."

After the meeting, I met individually with Brown. He offered to let me run my event at a later date and agreed to provide me with a letter of explanation for my sponsors and for the venue and local businesses that had interest in the event.

While at the Commissioners' meeting, I met a local promoter named Fred Rizzuto, who was willing to assist me in contracting local fighters to appear on my card. Fred had been running events in Massachusetts for five years, and during the prior year had promoted eleven events. For each of these events, he had to obtain approval for each fighter. For my event, he negotiated and signed contracts with fourteen licensed fighters.

The local staff was busy assisting in advertising and promoting the event. All of the details were falling into place when I became aware that Fred was having trouble getting approval from the Commission for the bouts that had been scheduled.

I asked Fred what the problem was, and he said, "Zeke, I don't know. I'm having trouble getting the contracts approved."

I reminded him that he told me that he just used these fighters recently on his own fight cards, and he replied, "I did, I got approval for all of them for my show." He said that he could not get approval from Cooper, and that he was getting frustrated.

"What the hell is Cooper trying to pull now?" I asked Fred, then continued, "Did he give you a reason?"

"No!" Fred replied, "He just said he's not going to approve those guys."

Fred was upset, and so was I. I had trouble understanding why he was having so much difficulty. After all, he was the most active promoter in the state.

The office staff, overhearing the phone call, asked me what the problem was. I looked at all of the people in my office and said, "I just don't know."

The staff understood that these were fighters who fought in Boston frequently, fighters who Fred had obtained approval for recently, and yet when he sub-

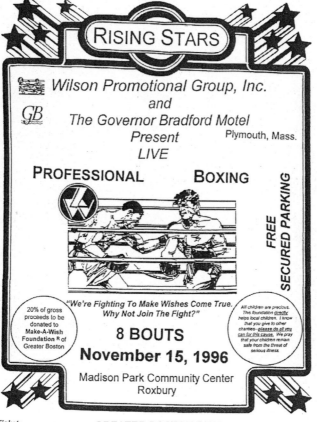

NEW ENGLAND'S FINEST

RISING STARS

Wilson Promotional Group, Inc.
and
The Governor Bradford Motel
Present   Plymouth, Mass.
LIVE

PROFESSIONAL   BOXING

FREE SECURED PARKING

PART OF EACH TICKET GOES TO THE MADISON PARK COMMUNITY CENTER
Show your support--tell your family and friends--help your community.
We need your support to bring more professional events to Roxbury.

20% of gross proceeds to be donated to Make-A-Wish Foundation ® of Greater Boston

All children are precious. This foundation directly helps local children. I know that you give to other charities--please do all you can for this cause. We pray that your children remain safe from the threat of serious illness.

"We're Fighting To Make Wishes Come True. Why Not Join The Fight?"

8 BOUTS
November 15, 1996

Madison Park Community Center
Roxbury

FEATURE : Darryl VS. Randy
BOUT : Johnson   McGee

IBO Inter-Continental Light Heavyweight Champion

Tickets

Golden Ringside:	$25
Ringside:	$20
General Admission:	$15

GREATER BOSTON FANS

You Have Seen the Rest
Now Watch the Best

Tickets Available at the Door, or in advance at
Madison Park Community Center
55 New Dudley Street
Roxbury

DOORS OPEN 6PM   FIRST BOUT 8PM

mitted their names to Cooper for my card, he just could not get them approved.

So I called Brown personally, and he told me that some of the fighters had their licenses suspended; some of them just couldn't fight. I told him that I knew that the fighters would not have signed contracts had they received notice of suspension and that these were Massachusetts fighters who fought regularly in Massachusetts.

Brown's response was that they were going to suspend the fighters at some point in the future. I told him that this was the craziest thing I had ever dealt with, and could not believe that they were pulling this crap. I had never in my life dealt with so many unreasonable demands. Brown said that he would have a conference with Cooper and would get back with me.

I also called Stan Cooper, and his excuse was that I had broken every rule of the Commission. Being frustrated, I threatened to sue them if they did not let me run my event, and Cooper's response was, "Go ahead. I love lawyers."

The next morning, Brown called me at 9:20 AM,

and informed me that the event was cancelled again, that I had broken every rule of the Commission and they would not let me proceed with the event.

Stunned, I hung up the phone and sat in shock on the edge of the bed. "Why are they doing this to me?" I wondered, out loud.

The answer that came to me was simple and true. "Because they feel they can."

Connie spoke with the manager at the Governor Bradford, Sherri Cochran, who said that she had already been contacted by Stan Cooper. He told Sherri that he would never let me run an event there.

It was clear at that point that there was nothing I could do, and that the best thing to do was to return to Pennsylvania to decide what course of action to take. The expense of promoting the event twice had depleted all working capital. I had obligations to the sponsors that I could not honor, and I also needed to try to find a way to salvage the plan that I had for expansion into other cities.

That same morning, we drove back to Pennsylvania. I arrived home penniless, exhausted, and angry. The feeling that you've worked so hard for so long to accomplish a goal, just to have everything snatched away by someone in a position of authority who misused their position to deprive you of your rights is a feeling that is difficult to describe and terrible to feel.

Besides the bank loan that we had obtained, I had sold four residential apartment units before going to Massachusetts. I had not owned the properties for too long, but wanted to pay off the mortgage and felt that I'd need what little equity I had to make things work in Massachusetts; and as it turns out, had I not been prevented from running the event, the money from the sale of the apartments would have made the difference in being able to advertise the second date, and the proceeds from the sale of tickets would have more than compensated.

Had I not been prevented.

We spent about a month gathering information. During that time, I consulted many attorneys, the general consensus of whom was to "chalk this one up to experience," because although the Commissioners clearly overstepped their authority, there was no way that they felt I could fight this battle and win. They felt that the cost of litigation alone would be excessive, even as much as one hundred thirty thousand dollars.

It didn't seem to matter to them when I complained that my constitutional rights were violated—most of them agreed with me unhesitatingly. But they also felt that dealing with the court system would not be to my advantage. Because there was *no precedent,* they felt that I wouldn't be able to prove discrimination, and that because the Commissioners held State positions, they were somehow above the law.

I stubbornly held my position, though, insisting that all citizens are entitled to basic rights, and that as a citizen I should receive protection under the Fourteenth Amendment.

Besides, the Commissioners' actions had hurt me too much. Still, I spoke with dozens of attorneys and could almost quote their response by this time--cost of litigation, burden of proof, state government position, years of litigation.

To an extent, all of them had the same concerns, but none of them disagreed about the fact that the Commissioners had no right to deprive me of doing business in Massachusetts after I had submitted to their procedures and followed all of their regulations.

"Every man, as long as he does not violate the laws of justice, is left perfectly free to pursue his own interest his own way, and to bring both his industry and capital into competition with those of any other man or order of men." -- Adam Smith

"While birds can fly, only humans can argue.
Argument is the affirmation of our being.
It is the principal instrument of human intercourse.
Without argument the species would perish.
As a subtle suggestion,
it is the means by which we aid another.
As a warning, it steers us from danger.
As exposition, it teaches.
As an expression of creativity,
it is the gift of ourselves.
As a protest, it struggles for justice.
As a reasoned dialogue, it resolves disputes.
As an assertion of self, it engenders respect.
As an entreaty of love, it expresses our devotion.
As a plea, it generates mercy.
As charismatic oration
it moves multitudes and changes history.
We must argue – to help, to warn, to lead, to love,
to create, to learn, to enjoy justice, to be."
Gerry Spence

"Constitutional rights may not be infringed simply because the majority of the people choose that they be."
Supreme Court of the United States

THE EIGHTH ROUND

"If our founding fathers, in 1776, had acknowledged the principle that a majority had the right to rule the minority, we should never have become a nation; for they were in a small minority, as compared with those who claimed the right to rule over them." -- Lysander Spooner

"If we aren't willing to pay a price for our values, then we should ask ourselves whether we truly believe in them at all." -- Barack Obama, The Audacity of Hope

"There can be no prescription old enough to supersede the Law of Nature and the grant of God Almighty, who has given to all men a natural right to be free, and they have it ordinarily in their power to make themselves so, if they please." -- James Otis

"The true test of the American ideal is whether we're able to recognize our failings and then rise together to meet the challenges of our time. Whether we allow ourselves to be shaped by events and history, or whether we act to shape them. Whether chance of birth or circumstance decides life's big winners and losers, or whether we build a community where, at the very least, everyone has a chance to work hard, get ahead, and reach their dreams."
Barack Obama, Speech, June 4, 2005

"I detest racialism, because I regard it as a barbaric thing, whether it comes from a black man or a white man."
Nelson Mandela

"It is easy to take liberty for granted, when you have never had it taken from you."
Dick Cheney

THE SIXTH ROUND:

◆———————◆

ON THE ROPES

I did not have enough money even to rent an apartment, and felt that I needed to stay in the area in order to find a way to take action against this injustice, so after we returned to Pennsylvania we stayed at Connie's mother's house for about a month. That was enough for me. The situation was not good.

With nowhere to go, Connie, Flo and I ended up staying at a homeless shelter. Flo was about two at the time. If you've never had occasion to visit a homeless shelter, you have no idea what that experience is like.

In the shelter, there was a large main room that served as the dining room, and during the daytime it became a recreation area for those who were not working or looking for work.

There was no provision for families to stay together. The men's dorm was a large, open room with rows of bunks. Due to their policy of turning no one away, in the dorm at any given time you could find someone with every physical and mental illness known to man. The dorm was seldom quiet, due to the variety of illnesses and the interrupted sleep of those with troubled minds.

The women's and children's dorm was upstairs, and after 8 PM families could not spend any time together until after 6:30 AM the following morning.

It took about a week before I had a job working in a local factory. Every spare moment, I would go to the public library to do research. Connie and Flo would accompany me every time. I told Connie that there was no way that I was going to let the Commissioners get away with the way that they deprived me of basic rights, so we needed to gather as much information as we could and make ourselves as familiar with the laws as possible.

In the meantime, I saved my money for an apartment. I found a part-time job managing a rooming house in the city, which gave my family a temporary home where we could be together. Soon the factory job ended, so managing the rooming house became my full-time job.

However, I realized that this was not an ideal situation for my family to be in. Because of the neighborhood that the rooming house was located in, there were problems inherent to the position. The complex housed people with all kinds of problems, ranging from drug use to dealing to prostitution. There were ongoing problems with people overdosing on all kinds of drugs, and both the police and FBI were frequent visitors. Still, I kept as much control over the situation as possible.

I knew that it would be best to move on quickly, and I still wanted to salvage my plan to train, manage and promote boxing. I saved enough money and in January of 1998, we moved to an area of North Central Pennsylvania that the locals call "God's Country", to Potter County, where there was enough seclusion and fresh air to make it an ideal location for a pro boxing camp.

The week after I moved my family, there was a gang war. The rooming house was shot up and burned, and was no longer inhabitable. Apparently, there were two rival gangs that were struggling for control of the complex and I was happy that I was no longer there.

The move also gave me time to renew my resolve to make a priority of handling the dispute with the Boxing Commission.

While compiling all of the information about the laws and issues, I tried numerous times to contact Fred Rizzuto. At first, Fred didn't want to take my calls, still upset that he had put so much time into the event without compensation.

After a while he was willing to talk and we had an interesting conversation. He told me that he heard from Tony Cornell and George Taylor, both of whom were active in boxing in the Boston area--and who told him that Cooper made some rather strong derogatory racial comments about me. He suggested that I should call them and see what they had to say.

Although we were all at the same meeting in October, I did not get to know either man. At Fred's recommendation I called George and introduced myself. I was amazed as he recounted to me that he had spoken with Stan Cooper at the meeting in October of '96. George said that not only did my name come up in the conversation, but that he was shocked by Cooper's attitude toward me as a Promoter.

George said that Cooper never intended to let me run events in Massachusetts. Cooper told him that he would "run that fucking Nigger out of town."

In fact, George was so offended by Cooper's comments that when he found out that Cooper did cancel my event, he wrote a letter to the Chairman of the Boxing Commission, to the Governor's office, and to the Department of Public Safety, reporting the conversation to them.

And now, over two years later, he was finally recounting the conversation to me. He went on to explain that he did meet with Brown after writing the letter, but he knew of no disciplinary action that was taken against Cooper.

I tried everything to convince the Commonwealth of Massachusetts to resolve the entire issue. On July 10 of '98 I compiled a brief three-page letter that summarized the issues and facts, and sent copies to the Boxing Commission, the Secretary of State, to the Governor, to the Department of Public Safety, and to Attorney General Gary Richmond.

After receiving no response from the Commonwealth of Massachusetts, I hired a Philadelphia attorney named Gordon Bey to write a letter in my behalf to the Commonwealth, informing the Department of Public Safety that a complaint would be filed if they did not resolve the issue.

We continued to call the Department of Public Safety, explaining the circumstances and trying to convince them that the Commissioners treated me wrongly and informing them that the Commissioners acted outside of the current laws and regulations to prevent me from doing business.

The Department of Public Safety decided to hold an internal investigation, and assigned Sam Covington to investigate. After about six months, the State decided to close the investigation, taking a stand, as they explained, that "they were of no opinion" regarding the matter.

At that point, I resumed looking for an attorney who would be willing to help me file a civil complaint. Numerous lawyers were sent a package containing copies of applicable Massachusetts Regulations and Statutes, fight cards and contracts.

The first thirty-five attorneys I spoke with felt that I had no chance. I even resorted to sending out postcards, hundreds of them, to attorneys to find one interested in taking on my case. We spoke with the NAACP and the ACLU, both of whom expressed sympathy with my plight, but neither of whom was equipped to handle a legal issue that was so specific to my situation.

Most of the attorneys who did respond to my postcards and phone calls quoted a high retainer along with their contingent fee, explaining that the cost and length of litigation, coupled with the chances of winning such a case, were so small that they could not take a risk. They felt that the cost to take the case to trial would be excessive, and doubted if it would even get to trial at all.

One day, I received a letter from Bob Hargrove, one of the attorneys in Boston that I'd been speaking with about filing the lawsuit. It contained a cover letter stating that he filed a complaint in Federal Court to protect my rights, along with a two-page complaint. For some of the issues, he felt that there may have been a two-year statute of limitations, and for other issues three years, and he didn't want me to lose my right to pursue all the issues.

Not being able to reach me, he took the initiative to file in my behalf. Although the complaint was filed improperly and would need to be amended, I appreciated his concern.

Upon receipt of his letter, I called Hargrove and he explained that the two of us would need to get together and review all of the documentation that I had, and to sign a representation agreement.

Hargrove explained during our meeting that he was not a trial attorney, but more of a negotiator.

The Defendants were being represented by the Massachusetts Attorney General's office. By state law the state had to indemnify state actors, and the Commissioners were state actors. Hargrove opened conversation with their office, feeling that it would be in my best interest to be reimbursed for my loss and have the state take some type of disciplinary action against the Commissioners. Then, he felt, I could get back to business as quickly as possible.

The Attorney General's office immediately filed a Motion to Dismiss, which the Court found in my favor, and discovery began.

I had already provided the State with initial discovery in the form of a packet of documents, fight cards, contracts and regulations and laws. The State responded by providing only one hundred eighteen pages of documents, many of which duplicated the information I had provided to them.

Hargrove also contacted Fred Rizzuto and scheduled his deposition, mostly to explore the merits of the case. Because he was unfamiliar with the facts, Hargrove asked for my assistance in compiling a list of questions and issues that would be important to the case.

During his deposition, Fred testified about the

difficulty he had in making matches for my card, his experience in putting together fights in Massachusetts, his experience with the Commissioners, and the normal procedures and time limits that were customarily imposed.

The Assistant Attorney General assigned to the case was John Kapinski. Kapinski tried to discredit Fred, but could not.

After the deposition, Hargrove and Kapinski spoke. Making sure that Kapinski understood my stand, Hargrove explained that if I were to be reimbursed for my loss and the Commissioners given disciplinary action, the suit would be dropped. Although Hargrove had done an able job of bringing out the issues, Kapinski felt that Brown's testimony would somehow magically overcome the facts.

Hargrove also scheduled depositions with George Taylor and Kevin Brown. The Attorney General's office called for my deposition.

Before taking George Taylor's deposition, I again supplied Hargrove with a list of questions and issues. In his deposition, George provided a copy of the letter he had sent to various persons and offices within the state.

This was the first time I had seen the actual letter, and I found it to be exactly as George had described on the phone. George verified the conversation he had with Cooper.

George also provided some background information on the Commissioners and on his experiences pertaining to the Commission's normal requirements for running an event.

After the deposition, Hargrove continued to try to negotiate with Kapinski, who still could not see a successful racial discrimination case.

Kapinski felt that in order to prevail, we would have to prove that the black Commission Chairman discriminated racially against me as a black Promoter.

But soon after George's deposition, a black promoter named Paul Johnson signed an affidavit on behalf of the defendants. Kapinski felt that the testimony of this black promoter, who was active in Massachusetts, would disprove Hargrove's argument.

Kapinski also felt that even if they acted wrongly, the Commissioners were entitled to qualified immunity because of the nature of their position.

Kapinski looked uncomfortable when Hargrove

questioned why the State had not produced a copy of George Taylor's letter along with the mandatory discovery documents required by the court—but Kapinski offered no answer or explanation.

He then offered Hargrove five hundred dollars as "nuisance pay" to resolve the complaint. He just could not see a successful case being tried before a jury where the plaintiff and the primary defendant were both race black.

Hargrove then called for the deposition of Kevin Brown. Brown held a PhD and was known for his gold-medal performance during the 1960 Olympic Games in Rome, Italy, when he successfully represented the United States Olympic Team along with Cassius Clay, better known as Muhammad Ali.

Hargrove lead Brown through a series of questions relating to his appointment to his position by the Governor, his understanding of the rules and regulations, and the oath that he took to uphold the laws of the Commonwealth.

Prior to Brown's deposition, Hargrove and Kapinski had numerous arguments regarding the laws that the complaint was filed under. Under sections

1981 and 1983 of the US Code, Kapinski still maintained that his clients were entitled to qualified immunity. Hargrove strongly disagreed, stating that "where there is racial animus, there is no qualified immunity."

Brown's deposition continued during the time that the disagreement between the attorneys was unanswered by the court, but would be addressed shortly afterwards.

The deposition lasted just over three hours, and Brown was true to form. He testified that he felt that he "could have and should have" prevented black promoters from running events in the state of Massachusetts.

He also defended his position by explaining that it takes money to run events and said, "It's not my fault that there's more money in the white pocket than in the black pocket."

He acknowledged that he was aware that the State law required a bond of five thousand dollars, that he required more of me, and that the only other person he required more of was the only other black promoter.

He also testified that he did receive George Taylor's letter, and although he didn't feel that the word

"Nigger" is derogatory, he claimed that he did speak with Cooper about it, but that no disciplinary action was taken.

Soon after Brown's deposition, Hargrove again spoke to Kapinski, who refused to raise his offer and filed a Motion to Dismiss with the court.

The main issues to be resolved in the motion were the Court's decision that the Defendants were entitled to no qualified immunity where the Plaintiff could prove racial animus, and although the Defendants attempted to have the case dismissed, Chief Justice Lloyd Travis agreed with my position that preventing me from running the events, thus acting outside of their inherent authority as Commissioners, was actionable under sections 1981 and 1983 of the US Code.

There was already, at this early stage of limited discovery and based upon Brown's deposition, enough indication of racial animus that the Court denied the Defendants' Motion to Dismiss, and ordered for discovery to continue.

Hargrove had gotten the feeling by this time that this was not a case that would be quickly settled, and following the Defendants' Motion to Dismiss, Hargrove withdrew from the case. That left me to proceed without representation.

◆———————◆

During the time after Hargrove's withdrawal when I was acting pro se, Chief Justice Travis recommended the case for non-binding arbitration, and I naively felt that, armed with the facts, the statutes and regulations, the justice presiding over the arbitration hearing was certain to see things my way and pressure the Attorney General's office to agree to a reasonable resolution.

I remembered that once, Hargrove and I had a conversation about Robinson, who was serving as the ADR judge. Hargrove gave him a high review, saying, "Judge Robinson is indeed a professional. I remember once, I had a case that was already lost at trial, and the case was being appealed. The defendants did not want to settle, so Judge Robinson asked me to leave the room."

Hargrove continued, "Keeping the defendants and their attorney in conference, after about forty-five minutes the case settled for the amount that the Judge had suggested."

So I drove to Boston with high hopes, entertaining

the vision that I would come home reimbursed for my loss, and with the satisfaction that the state would take disciplinary action against the Commissioners. Sometimes you can visualize the way a set of circumstances will unfold, step by step, and can be so close to the eventual reality. But this was not one of those instances!

I learned very quickly that the ADR judge, Robinson, had only one objective. It was to end as many cases as possible and clear them from the Court's docket. Granted, it is expensive to run a court room, but I had expected ADR to be a miniature version of the trial, a presentation of the facts where the Arbitrator would apply his years of knowledge and wisdom to help the parties decide a reasonable outcome.

Judge Robinson listened to each side for about ten minutes, and recommended that the Defendants pay five thousand dollars as liquidated damages, with no admission of liability. I was probably wasting my breath explaining to Robinson that the issue was one of rights—I had followed the laws and regulations at all times, had submitted to licensing procedure, and still was prevented from exercising the right to run events.

Robinson argued with me, taking a position that had I not been prevented, and had my event proceeded, there was no guarantee that the event would have made a profit.

I found myself feeling insulted and getting very angry, but allowed him to continue. Robinson explained that there were guys who graduated from law school with him who were driving cabs for a living—his point being that there were no guarantees of income in life.

I took a long, deep breath, and in the calmest voice I could muster, pointed out that while that may be true, it would have been different had they been prevented from attending college in the first place because of some arbitrary decision based on their skin color or their ancestry.

Having reached an impasse, I left the hearing and returned home, spending the eight-hour drive reviewing the day's events and feeling that the entire trip was a waste of time.

THE EIGHTH ROUND

"The true test of the American ideal is whether we're able to recognize our failings and then rise together to meet the challenges of our time. Whether we allow ourselves to be shaped by events and history, or whether we act to shape them. Whether chance of birth or circumstance decides life's big winners and losers, or whether we build a community where, at the very least, everyone has a chance to work hard, get ahead, and reach their dreams." --
Barack Obama
Speech, June 4, 2005

"For all things difficult to acquire, the intelligent man works with perseverance."
Lao Tzu

"Those who know the truth are not equal to those who love it."
Confucius

"The essence of our effort to see that every child has a chance must be to assure each an equal opportunity, not to become equal, but to become different - to realize whatever unique potential of body, mind and spirit he or she possesses" -- John Fischer

"In the end, we will remember not the words of our enemies, but the silence of our friends."
Rev. Dr. Martin Luther King, Jr.

"The best principles of our republic secure to all its
citizens a perfect equality of rights."
Thomas Jefferson

"Nothing in this world can take the place of persistence.
Talent will not; nothing is more common than
unsuccessful people with talent.
Genius will not; unrewarded genius is almost a proverb.
Education will not; the world is full of educated derelicts.
Persistence and determination alone are omnipotent.
The slogan "press on" has solved and always will solve
the problems of the human race"
Calvin Coolidge

"Today the choice is no longer between violence and
nonviolence. It is either nonviolence or nonexistence."
Rev. Dr. Martin Luther King, Jr.
1964, Stride Towards Freedom

"Victory belongs to the most persevering."
Napoleon Bonaparte

"Permanence, perseverance and persistence in spite of all
obstacles, discouragement, and impossibilities:
It is this that in all things distinguishes
the strong soul from the weak"
Thomas Carlyle

We didn't all come over on the same ship,
but we're all in the same boat."
Bernard M. Baruch

"Before God we are all equally wise
and equally foolish."
Albert Einstein

"The things that will destroy us are: politics without
principle; pleasure without conscience;
wealth without work; knowledge without character;
business without morality; science without humanity; and
worship without sacrifice."
Mahatma Mohandas K. Gandhi

"It is not my intention to do away with government, but
rather to make it work—work with us, not over us; to
stand by our side, not ride on our back. Government can
and must provide opportunity, not smother it; foster
productivity, not stifle it… How can we love our country
and not love our countrymen, and loving them, not reach
out a hand when they fall, heal them when they are sick,
and provide opportunities to make them self-sufficient so
they will be equal in fact and not just in theory?"
Ronald Reagan

THE SEVENTH ROUND:

———◆————◆———

ALMOST OUT

In the fall of 1999, the Defendants filed another motion to dismiss the case. They had tried twice to schedule my deposition, and I tried to hold them off until I could find an attorney to represent me.

At the time, I was making arrangements to meet an attorney named Brian Green out of Southern Pennsylvania, and was hoping to make the six-hour drive to meet with him and to retain him to finish the discovery and take the case to trial.

After I signed a representation agreement with him, we called Kapinski and convinced him to agree to rescind his motion to dismiss. Kapinski filed a request to rescind the pending motion, not knowing at the time that Judge Travis granted his motion the same morning. Under the Court Rules, a motion may be rescinded by the moving party at any time prior to notification of the Order. Since the Court had not sent out notification of the Order, the request to rescind the pending motion superseded the Order, and the case was reinstated. So we were out and back within a day!

Brian Green was counsel of record for a few brief months. Like Hargrove, he felt that the case would settle quickly, but that was not to be. When the State produced arguments that they had treated white promoters the same way, and that the other black promoter in the state had no problems with the Commission, he could not see a way to argue effectively.

I could not convince Green of the value of seeing

the case through to trial, and although the State made no significant offer, I could not agree with his opinion, even when speaking hypothetically. Green felt that if he could get the state to offer fifteen thousand dollars, I should, in his words, "Take it and run."

We quickly developed a personality clash, neither of us being willing to bend to the other's will. Green often told me, "You believe in the fairy tale of being able to tell your story in court. You will never, *ever* tell your story in a court of law." He assured me that I would never get to tell my story in a courtroom, because he felt that the state would win in a summary judgment motion.

Therefore, Green felt that it would be best to take *any* offer from the State. As the date approached for the State to take my deposition, Green filed a request with the Court to withdraw as counsel. I filed a motion of opposition with the Court, and argued that Green should stay until replacement counsel was found. I felt that it was a delicate time in the progress of the case to be without legal advice, even if we did not see eye to eye.

It was on the morning of my deposition that I

waited for Green at the State Office building, and it was finally John Kapinski who informed me that the Judge had granted Green's motion to withdraw as counsel. Apparently, Green had never filed for pro hac vice, and so technically he never represented me before the Court; therefore, the Court could not make Green continue.

So, ten minutes before my deposition I found that I was once again on my own, without counsel. My deposition lasted all day, with a few brief breaks. I would have preferred legal advice, but as I was there to simply tell the truth, it went exceptionally well. To this day, I keep a copy of the three-hundred-page deposition transcript and pick it up from time to time to give it a quick look.

It was customary to receive regular emails from Kapinski every few days. Occasionally, he would email informing me of information or to schedule the many conferences and meetings required by the Court. More often than not, though, his emails were designed to raise my blood pressure, and we often got into "a war of words."

The State had produced only one hundred eighteen pages of discovery documents, even after a request for document copies on a wide area of applicable subjects—licensed promoters, events, approved bouts, etc. The Judge had ruled for the State to produce the documentation requested, and in lieu of their production of documents, granted permission for me to view and copy the documents during normal business hours at their offices.

So when I received an email from Kapinski late one afternoon informing me that he would be leaving for a vacation in Hawaii the next day, I packed my bags and drove late that night to Boston.

At 9 AM, I was at the office of the Boxing Commission, Judge's Order for document production in my hand, and informed the front desk that I was there to view and reproduce documents. The receptionist escorted me to the office of the Department of Public Safety, and introduced me to a man named Patrick Reed, who tried his best to convince me that I would need to make an appointment for a later date.

I visualized the entire office watching me leave and then scurrying about like ants, carrying stacks of documents to a secure hiding place, never to be seen again. There was no way that I could let that happen!

I showed Reed the Court Order, stating that the documents could be viewed and photocopied during normal business hours. Reed tried repeatedly to call Kapinski, who I imagined at the time was either on a flight for the West Coast, or waiting for a connecting flight, or maybe even crossing the Pacific toward Hawaii. In any case, he could not be reached.

Reed laid the phone down and began to explain his decision to schedule another time for me to come back. I countered by explaining that the Judge would certainly be happy to enjoin him as a defendant should he wish to prevent the enforcement of the Order.

That must not have been a position he wished to be in, and so for the next five days he and his administrative assistant spent four hours per day with us as we carried the complete set of files of the Boxing Commission into a conference room, combed through every page of every file, flagged the pages we wanted to copy with Post Its, and waited while his assistant took the files to the copy room.

By this time, Brown and Cooper both had been dismissed as Commissioners, the newly appointed Commissioners did not know what we were looking for, and Kapinski was still unavailable.

Each day, we carried hundreds of pages back with us—by taxi to the train station, and an hour and a half to Bellingham, the western-most stop on the commuter train. We would spend the evening reviewing documents at a small motel near the train station, and be back on the train again at 7 AM to repeat the day.

By the end of the week, we had finished reviewing files and were on our way back home.

Having collected literally thousands of pages of documents, the task ahead was to organize and analyze the information into a comprehensive collection of information that could be used convincingly to my benefit in speaking before a jury.

There were a few glaring discrepancies between Brown's deposition testimony and the documents uncovered. The first was the lack of bonding—any bonding—with a few disturbing exceptions.

The second was the apparent lack of anything to

support the Commission's claim of invoking a ten-day rule.

I knew that any issue that was not absolute would give the Defendants room to "wiggle" into an explanation that the jury just might buy. I would need to have all of my details in order, backed up by documents of the Commission, in order to gain the agreement of the jury.

I needed to be able to prove to a jury that I was treated differently than promoters who were not black, and I needed to be able to prove to a jury that the Boxing Commission, headed by a Chairman who was also black, discriminated against me. All of this without *any precedent* in Federal Court for same-race discrimination.

At this point, we were comfortable with being able to convince a jury of the bond issue. The documentation was specific. Of the two dozen promoters licensed by the Boxing Commission during the tenure of these Commissioners, and despite the State law, which had not changed during the time, there were exactly three promoters who needed a bond at all.

I was one, Don King was the second, and Paul Johnson was the third. We were the only three black promoters. No white promoter was required to post any bond at all. Not even the one required by law. The defendants had no room to wiggle on that one!

Likewise, there was no HIV regulation that legally gave them the right to require testing.

One issue that would need to be overcome was the Commissioners' contention that the bouts I submitted for my fight card were not good bouts, and that they could not in good conscience give approval for the bouts. Then, it was a simple step to disallow the event for failure to have enough bouts approved for the card. It is harder to overcome an argument based on judgment than one based on facts.

The second issue dealt with the Commissioners' cancellation of the event of a white promoter, supposedly for the same reasons. From the original discovery materials, the Defendants provided documentation to support their contention that they did prevent a white promoter, Dennis Smith, from running an event and suspended his promoter's license for failure to submit an approved fight card ten days before an event. They provided a copy of the letter from the Commissioners notifying him that his license would be suspended. When I copied documents, I also found minutes of a meeting of the Commissioners where they discussed taking disciplinary action against Smith.

This issue would be the final one to put to rest in the preparation for trial. To make the issue more complicated, the defendants took an affidavit from the other black promoter, Paul Johnson, which stated that he never had a problem with the Commission or with any of the Commissioners.

With these issues firmly in mind, Kapinski filed his final Motion for Summary Judgment, hoping that the judge would agree with him that there just was not enough evidence to support my contention of racial discrimination, for the case to continue to a trial before a jury, and so dismiss the case.

I called quite a few attorneys and asked how a person goes about objecting to the summary judgment. That's when I became aware of how important this document would be, as one attorney after another painted a picture of the Summary Judgment being the life- or death-sentence of a case.

Line by line, we picked apart Kapinski's motion, word by word, and made a list of the facts that he contended, marking which ones were factually incorrect and which ones we had proof to negate. It took us days to analyze the document, and armed only with high-school educations and the will to see it through, we began preparing an opposition to the motion.

The Assistant Attorney General told me that I never stood a chance. He reminded me that I had trouble keeping the confidence of the attorneys that I had representing me. That's why I was preparing the opposition by myself.

As a pro se Plaintiff, I also understood that had I forgotten just one issue that the Defense raised, had I not been able to convince the Judge that there was sufficient evidence on every issue, the case would not proceed.

I remembered every attorney I had ever spoken with, and their opinions would ring in my ears.

They felt that the court would never see discriminatory behavior when the Plaintiff and the leading Defendant were both race black. They felt that the State would produce too much evidence that would either distort the truth to the jury, or paint a picture of public servants doing their best in their position, and the jury would side with the Defendants out of sympathy. They said that I would never win. They said that I would never make it to trial.

In the midst of all of this, I also remembered Mama's voice coming back from all those years before, encouraging me to never give up. All of this was going through my mind as I prepared a twenty-one page opposition to the summary judgment motion. Finally feeling that I had responded to all of the Attorney General's issues and in addition had stated my case, I put the finishing touches on the opposition and printed it out to file with the Court.

Then came the waiting. I filed the opposition in the middle of May of 2000. This had to be one of the scariest moments in the entire case. I could see the entire argument clearly, and knew first-hand that the Commissioners were wrong. At the same time, waiting for the Judge to make a determination was one of the most intense waiting periods that I'd ever had, and I called the Court daily to find out if the order had been filed yet.

Finally, the Judge called for a hearing to determine the Summary Judgment, and I made the trip to Boston once again, confident of the facts but nervous about the outcome of the hearing. In my heart, I believed in the American judicial system, and wanted to give justice a chance to prevail.

At that point, I was reluctant to even talk to attorneys. No attorney believed that I would prevail, although there were some who congratulated me for taking the issue as far as I had. Numerous promoters, boxers, trainers, and managers in Massachusetts were all at the edges of their seats, waiting for the outcome and knowing what had happened.

To this day, I remember clearly every word of the Summary Judgment hearing. The Judge reviewed the highlights of the documents filed by both sides, and I noted how meticulous Judge Travis was to detail. It was up to this one man to decide if what I believed would go forward, or if in his opinion it did not merit consideration before a jury.

I listened to Kapinski argue that there was nothing to indicate racial animus on the part of the Commissioners. Then I directed him to the quotes from Brown's deposition, comments made under oath that constituted racial animus. The Judge agreed that the comments were indeed indicative of derogatory racial remarks.

I looked directly into the Judge's eyes, and listened to every word carefully. There was the issue of a third commissioner, Dave Brookfield, whom Hargrove had initially named in the complaint but was not really involved directly in the events that happened. There was also no documentation to support that he was directly involved, so when the Judge questioned whether he should remain as a Defendant, I told the judge that I had no objection to releasing his name from the case.

Judge Travis turned to Kapinski, and told him that this case would go to trial. Then he turned to me, and explained that he felt that I did an excellent job so far, but this was a complicated case and he advised me that it would be best for me to find an attorney to take the case to trial.

Little did he know that I had been looking for an attorney the whole time! Even so, I felt that I would burst as I thanked the Judge and walked from the courtroom, feeling like there was nothing I could not accomplish.

Following the hearing, I stood on the wharf next to the McDonalds that was in the entrance level of the courthouse. Kapinski admitted that if I could argue in court the way I argued on paper, I would have a chance. He still felt that Johnson was his ace, and that with his testimony the jury would be made to see that there was no racial animus, and that the Commissioners must have had some other problem with the event, or with me.

Kapinski was interested in who I might get to represent me for trial. I did not want to tell him that I had no clue who I would be able to get, but feeling that having survived summary judgment was enough for now, I took a series of long, deep breaths and hoped that it would also make a difference and be easier to convince an attorney now that it was actually going to trial.

I took a taxi back to the train station, trying to think of which attorney I might be able to speak with and convince. We were about to catch the commuter train back to Bellingham, where I had parked, when I reached Harry Miller on the phone. It was now about 5:30 PM, and I was surprised that we reached him so late in the afternoon. I told Harry that the case survived summary judgment, and he couldn't believe it. He said that if I could come over to his office, he would take time to discuss the case that evening.

Following our discussion, Harry agreed to take a look at all the documents. He still had major reservations because he did not think that a jury would see racial discrimination with a black chairman as Defendant. There was absolutely no precedent for same-race discrimination anywhere in the federal court records.

However, over the course of the next few weeks I continued to speak with him on the phone, trying to convince him that we could win. It did not help that in Judge Travis's court, it had been about three years, to his knowledge, since a Plaintiff had won a case. Perhaps he finally decided that he would have little to lose in terms of expenses and time. After looking at the pretrial memorandum, he made a commitment to handle the trial.

One day, as the phone rang insistently, Connie entered the living room, with Flo following behind her. Reaching for the phone, she answered, "Hello?"

A man with an unfamiliar, gravely voice answered, "If you know what's good for you, you'll drop your case, bitch."

She asked, "Who is this?" But there was no response, only a dial tone. Looking momentarily confused, she shrugged then hung up the phone.

Flo asked, "Mommy, was that Daddy on the phone?"

Looking puzzled, Connie answered, "No, your Daddy is at work. It was just someone playing with the phone."

Flo replied, "Their mommy is going to get mad. I'm going outside to ride my bike now."

"Not until you have lunch," Connie corrected.

"Then can I go out and ride my bike?" Flo asked.

Connie nodded and carried two plates to the table. As soon as Flo finished her lunch, she hurried outside, Connie following close behind her. As the door closed, the phone began to ring again.

Connie yelled, "Be careful! Stay in the yard, I'll be right back."

Flo replied, "Okay, Mommy."

Still watching Flo through the window, Connie reached again for the phone. "Hello?"

The same voice answered her again, saying, "You better not ever come back to Boston, you Nigger-loving bitch."

Connie shouted, "Stop calling here."

The man's voice continued, "Fuck you, you Nigger-loving bitch."

Connie hung up the phone, obviously upset by the call, and at about the same time I arrived home from work.

"Is everything okay?" I asked.

"Yeah, why do you ask?" Connie replied, trying to act cheerful.

I said, "It seemed strange that you'd let Flo ride bike by herself." I wasn't buying the cheerful act, so I asked, "What's wrong?"

Connie replied, "I came back in the house to

answer the phone."

"But are you okay?" I asked.

She said, "Yes, I'm just tired." She explained that she had been working on the documents for Harry and was pretty much finished. Then she explained that she had some prank calls.

I responded by asking her, "What did they say?"

She said that they were talking crazy stuff, racial stuff. I was just replying, "So that's what's wrong with you," when the phone rang again.

Connie watched me as I picked up the phone, and said, "Hello."

The voice on the other end said, "You better not ever come back to Boston, Nigger, you and that white bitch you got."

I demanded, "Who is this?"

The voice replied, "You're going to lose, you fucking Nigger, you and your white bitch-ass wife."

By this time, I was extremely upset and said, "Whoever you are, you can go to hell." I abruptly hung up the phone and looked at Connie.

She said that someone was calling here all day, and walked over to the door. She called to Flo, "You need to come inside now!"

"Okay, Mom." Flo answered and she began to park her bike.

I walked over behind Connie, who was still standing in the open doorway. I put my hands on her shoulders and said, "There are people who never thought we'd get this far."

Flo finished parking her bike and began to climb the steps toward the front door. She said, "Hi, Dad. How was your day?"

I replied, "My day was good."

"Hey, Dad," she continued, "I was riding my bike all by myself!"

I said, "That's good."

Later that evening, I sat watching television. Connie entered the darkened living room and joined me on the couch. I said to her, "You're shaking."

She replied, "I'm okay."

I looked at her and asked, "Are you still thinking about that phone call?"

She tried to appear cheerful again, as she said, "No, but that guy was creepy, and we've been getting hang-ups for months."

I asked her, "Then why does it bother you so much now?"

She said to me, "They're not just hanging up anymore, now that we're going to trial."

I told her, "If people are upset about what we're doing, I just don't care."

Connie looked at me for a few moments, then said, "Sometimes I wonder if they stopped you because you're black—*or because I'm white*?"

"What are you saying? Those people are just ignorant!" was my reply.

Connie wasn't dissuaded so easily. She continued, "Zeke, you just don't know. What if they did stop you because I'm white? What about the judge? What about the jury? How are they going to look at us?"

Trying to calm her, I replied, "Don't worry…"

But she interrupted, asking, "How can I not worry?

Would this have even happened if I was black?"

My tone got serious, as I told her, "Connie, listen. These people are racist. They would have done this anyway. This isn't because of you and it isn't because you're white."

"But how do you know?" she asked, and continued, "I never had to deal with anything like this before!"

I tried again to calm her by saying, "Trial will be over soon."

She replied, somewhat sadly, "But this will *never* be over. People will always be ignorant and hateful."

"Maybe," I said, "I can't promise that people won't stare or talk about us." I continued, saying, "Lots of families deal with the same thing. Just remember, all we can do is to be strong and raise our daughter the right way."

As I was speaking, I began to pull her closer, and said, "Besides, if everyone that this happened to would stand up and fight this injustice, things would change."

"So," she said, "You don't blame me?"

I replied, "No way."

THE SEVENTH ROUND:
Almost Out

We arrived early for the pretrial hearing, because we had to file the pretrial documents. I stopped by the clerk's office and then headed to the courtroom. Kapinski was there, gloating that I had not yet been able to find an attorney.

Although I had not seen Harry that morning, I was sure that he would be there as promised, and I looked around as I sat in the courtroom. The judge would be holding the hearing in his chambers, and Kapinski went in to make himself comfortable. Kapinski was an excellent attorney, very sharp and skilled at his job, and even at this late point, he was continuing to tell me that he would try to get the case thrown out.

As he was taunting me about my lack of procedural skills, Harry Miller walked into the courtroom. Kapinski looked dazed, and Harry enthusiastically shook his hand! Seeing Kapinski's confusion, he pulled a copy of the appearance notice—which he had faxed to Kapinski's office that morning—out of his briefcase, and handed it to Kapinski.

The look on Kapinski's face was priceless, as he angrily threw the papers into his briefcase and stormed out into the hallway to use his cell phone. I imagined that he was on the phone with the Attorney General, cursing me for having retained such skilled counsel at this late date.

At the end of the pretrial conference, both sides were informed that the trial was scheduled to begin in only ten days. Although I had planned and budgeted for a one-day trip for the conference, Harry explained that he needed me to stay in Boston until after the trial was over, so that we could prepare.

I spent the week with Harry, helping him review and become familiar with all of the facts, organizing a strategy for presenting the documents to the jury, and ordering records of Massachusetts events. Denise Collins, who helped organize and prepare documents for presentation to the jury, assisted Harry with the trial.

She also proved to be skilled at investigation, and she uncovered a discrimination complaint that Johnson had filed two years before. The complaint would be valuable to disprove Johnson's claim that he never had any occasion to feel that he had been discriminated against.

The week went quickly, and jury selection would

begin promptly at 9 AM on Monday. I anxiously anticipated the trial that took four long years to finally arrive, and at 8 AM was ready to leave the train station to make the ten-minute cab ride to the McCormick Federal courthouse on Fan Pier.

Even though the driver insisted that he knew the way, between traffic and construction detours, the ten-minute taxi ride lasted over an hour. It was 9:15 when we finally walked into the Courtroom, and I could see that Harry and Denise were pacing and wondering how I could be late.

As it turned out, though, Chief Justice Travis was also delayed, and I wasn't there for more than two minutes when I heard the bailiff shout, "All Rise."

Jury selection was an interesting process. It began with about twenty-four potential jurors, and the Judge spoke with the group to determine if any of them had prior knowledge of the case or of any of the parties. He briefly explained that this would be a trial to determine if racial discrimination had in fact occurred, and if so to determine what award should be given.

After excusing a few jurors who felt that they could

not be unbiased, and a few who because of the expected length of the trial could not serve, about twenty were left. Twelve of the twenty were randomly selected to fill the jury seats, and each attorney had an opportunity to excuse a few jurors. The vacant seats were then filled by random selection, and the attorneys had the opportunity to again excuse a few more jurors.

Finally, there were twelve jurors and after a brief recess, trial would begin. My greatest concern was that there was just so much information, an overwhelming mountain of documents, and uncountable facts that they would be giving to the jury and asking them to absorb in such a brief period of time.

I asked myself if I would have been able to absorb it all, had the information been new to me as it would be to these twelve men and women.

That's when I noticed just how full the courtroom was. Every seat was taken, and there were about thirty people standing.

Harry saw me looking, and explained that my case was a topic of discussion in the law schools at both Harvard and Yale, and that many students would attend to observe. Others were civil rights litigators who had tremendous interest in the precedent that the case would set.

"I would remind you that extremism in the defense of liberty is no vice! And let me remind you also that moderation in the pursuit of justice is no virtue."
Barry Goldwater

"Like and equal are two entirely different things."
Madeleine L'Engle, A Wrinkle in Time

"My political ideal is democracy. Let every man be respected as an individual and no man idolized."
Albert Einstein
Ideas And Opinions, Page 9 (The World As I See It)

"Education is the passport to the future, for tomorrow belongs to those who prepare for it today."
Malcolm X

"I am leaving this legacy to all of you ... to bring peace, justice, equality, love and a fulfillment of what our lives should be. Without vision, the people will perish, and without courage and inspiration, dreams will die-- the dream of freedom and peace."
Rosa Parks

"If you prick us, do we not bleed? if you tickle us, do we
not laugh? if you poison us, do we not die? and if you
wrong us, shall we not revenge?"
William Shakespeare
Source: The Merchant of Venice- Act III, Scene I

"An enlightened person - by perceiving God in all - looks
at a learned person, an outcast, even a cow, an elephant, or
a dog with an equal eye."
Bhagavad Gita 5.18

"We hold these truths to be self evident, that all (people)
are created equal; that they are endowed by their Creator
with certain unalienable rights, that among these are life,
liberty and the pursuit of happiness."
The Declaration of Independence

"To live anywhere in the world today and be against
equality because of race or color, is like living in Alaska
and being against snow."
William Faulkner

"We are a nation of many nationalities, many races, many
religions bound together by a single unity, the unity of
freedom and equality."
Franklin D. Roosevelt

Do not follow where the path may lead. Go, instead,
where there is no path and leave a trail.
Ralph Waldo Emerson

THE EIGHTH ROUND:

$$\blacklozenge \!\!-\!\!-\!\!-\!\!-\!\!-\!\!-\!\!-\!\!-\!\!\blacklozenge$$

THE FINAL BELL

As soon as the recess was over, both attorneys gave their opening arguments. I intently watched the jury, trying to read them. Over the course of the next week, I'd find that some of them were expressive, others weren't. I tried to gauge their reactions, to figure out where they stood.

Harry took the opportunity to inform the jury that

over the course of the next few days, he would present overwhelming evidence, much of it the Commissions' own documents, to prove beyond the shadow of a doubt that I had been treated disparately by the Defendant Commissioners.

He explained that the Defendants regularly followed one set of operating procedures for white promoters, and required more of black promoters. He also explained that the Defense would try to convince them that because the Chairman of the Commission was a black man, it would be impossible for racial discrimination to occur.

He thanked them for taking time out of their everyday lives to serve, and asked only that they keep an open mind and pay attention to the myriad of facts that would be presented.

Kapinski's opening argument was that the event was cancelled by the Commissioners, not because of racial discrimination and not through any wrong action of the Commissioners, but because of a lack of organization of the event; and furthermore, when white promoters broke rules of the Commission, their events were likewise cancelled by the same Commissioners.

Immediately following the opening arguments, Judge Travis turned the trial over to Harry, who called me as the first witness. I spent the rest of the first day and all of the second day on the stand, testifying and being cross-examined. Most of my testimony was factual, painting a picture for the jury of the events as they unfolded.

Cross-examination consisted mainly of Kapinski asking me the same questions I had already answered in my deposition, worded differently, to see if my answers would change. Any difference in my answers could be used by the Defense to try to make me appear dishonest or unsure of the events.

Each day, when Court recessed for the day, I would go to Harry's office to prepare for the next day and discuss the effect of the day's testimony. Each evening, I would take the commuter train back to Bellingham, then drive to Woonsocket, Rhode Island, where I was staying.

It's odd how, in a city with millions of inhabitants, people keep such regular schedules. Over the week of trial preparation, I kept the same schedule and rode the commuter train with the same people, and as I became familiar with these men and women, they began to listen to my conversations with Connie, asking how the day went, discuss the issues and testimony, and offer moral support.

So, as I got onto the train at the end of the first day, it did not feel unusual when everyone asked how the day went. I was discussing the jury selection with my wife, that it seemed odd that in a city of such diversity, I would end up with a jury composed entirely of white men and women.

We came to an agreement, though, that the circumstances would touch the hearts of people who may have never experienced discrimination first-hand, and we had faith in the eventual outcome.

We discussed the jurors individually. The fore-woman, who was a schoolteacher, listened intently and took a lot of notes. She seemed to pay a lot of attention to details, and we felt that she would not miss the facts and the merits of the documentation.

Most of the other jurors were somewhat easy to read—they were expressive and nodded in agreement at times.

There was one juror, though, who was impossible to read. A union construction worker, he sat in the middle of the back row, and he showed no emotion or reaction at all.

My travel mates listened carefully as I discussed the day's events. They listened as Connie expressed that the jury seemed to really connect well with me as I was on the stand, and they all seemed genuinely interested in the facts before them.

I spent the entire second day continuing my testimony, finishing recounting the facts to the Court.

The Defendants must have also noticed how intently the jury was listening, and so they began making audible comments, disagreeing with my account of the facts. As Brown loudly laughed and shook his head, Cooper made a final hiss, "He's lying!"

Finally, the Judge had heard enough, and he interrupted the proceedings. In a raised voice, Judge Travis said, *"That's enough!* I'll have order! If I hear one more word, I'll have you removed from this court. Do I make myself clear? Mr. Miller, you may proceed."

I was somewhat surprised at the level of emotion he displayed, and wondered if two years of pleadings had caused him to form his own opinion about the case.

When I was finished on the witness stand, the Judge called a recess until the next morning.

On Wednesday, Harry called George Taylor, Fred Rizzuto, and Connie to the stand.

Fred testified about his past experience with the Commissioners, the normal procedure and his success rate for bout approval. He explained to the jury his background and his experience with the Commission— and his frustration at not being able to get approval for any of the fighters he contracted for this event. He explained that this is something that he had a good deal of experience and success with, and yet, when he called Cooper with the same fighters for this card, the bouts were not approved.

In addition to not approving suitable bouts, Cooper also phoned at least two of the fighters, Ron White and Donny Snyder, and told them not to fight on my card.

Next, George Taylor testified about his conversation with Cooper four years before, and about the letter of complaint that he wrote even before he met me. The jury listened intently when George explained that it was before the second cancellation when Cooper told him that he would never let me run an event, and the jurors all took note when he read the letter that he had written and distributed, in which he quoted Cooper as saying about me, *"I will run that fuckin' Nigger out of town."*

Although I didn't know the men, I felt so much respect for both Fred and George, knowing that they must have been under tremendous pressure from the Commission, which they still dealt with on an ongoing basis. They had nothing to gain personally from their testimony, and yet they were willing to endure the consequences of coming forward.

I admired the courage of good people like these men, and the men and women of the jury, who spend valuable time and effort to help correct a situation even though it doesn't directly affect them.

Finally, Harry called Connie to the stand. As he lead her through an explanation of the documents that we'd found during discovery and the analysis tables she prepared from them, Kapinski objected to entry of the documents as exhibits.

Kapinski knew by that time how damaging the documents would be, and he raised an objection, stating, "Your Honor, the copier at the State offices had broken down, and some of the documents were not copied and forwarded to Mr. Wilson until after the discovery period was over. In fact, he did not receive the balance of the copied material until after the pretrial conference. Therefore, I feel that the documents should not be admissible."

The Judge overruled the objection, mainly because in the interim between the time the documents were marked for copying and the time I received the copies, the documents were at the State office, in the control and custody of the Defendants at all times, and so the Defendants had constant access to them.

I breathed a sigh of relief, knowing that the documentation was important in establishing facts about the procedures of the Commission.

In addition, I needed to disprove every excuse that the Defendants could offer to defend their actions. In the pleadings, Brown made reference to an issue of the finances of promoters as an excuse for the bond requirement in excess of the statutory amount.

In the Commission's files, there were over two hundred pages of promoter's applications. In all of the files of the Commission there were only three promoters who were ever actually required to get a bond, and only three bonds. They were issued on behalf of Paul Johnson, Don King, and Zeke Wilson. Now, although both Paul Johnson and I were of fairly modest finances, Don King supplied the Commission with a balance sheet demonstrating a net worth in excess of thirteen million dollars.

On the other hand, white promoters also submitted financial reports with their applications. Even in the case of applicants who had a net worth of fifteen hundred dollars, no bond had been required—not even the statutory one.

The documents were essential for issues such as these, where not only did they enforce requirements more strictly for me than they had the authority to, but in contrast actually were more lax in their requirements for white promoters than their authority demanded. I watched the reaction of the jurors closely as these issues were presented.

Connie's testimony continued for the rest of the day, and when Court recessed, she would be resuming the next day. After she finished late Thursday morning, Kapinski began calling witnesses.

The first witness called to the stand was Kevin Brown. Brown painted a picture of me as a non-resident who wanted to promote boxing events, who broke the rules and procedures of the Commission and then tried to blame the Commissioners because of ignorance of the laws. Brown repeatedly stated, *"ignorance of the law is no excuse,"* and explained to the jury that he, "as a black man, would never permit racial discrimination in *my* Commission."

He was also very happy to report that Dennis Smith, a white promoter, had scheduled an event that was cancelled by the Commission for failure to follow Commission rules. In fact, Kapinski had photocopied documents that clearly showed that the Commission cancelled Smith's event and suspended his promoter's license for failure to follow the rules and policies of the Commission.

This was the only time during the entire trial that evidence was actually distributed directly to the jury. I watched in amazement as the fabricated document was passed out to each juror individually, as positive proof that they were only using the same standard for me that they used for white promoters.

As Kapinski rested, Harry leaned toward me and said, "I'm going to eat this guy up!"

After having Brown recount his appointment to the position of Chairman by the Governor, and the oath he took to uphold the laws of the Commonwealth of Massachusetts, the procedure for legally changing the regulations, and the importance and effect of acting outside of the laws and regulations, Harry lead both Brown and the jury through a quick review of the regulations that were actually in effect in November of '96.

Brown had testified during his deposition that he understood that he had taken an oath to uphold the laws that pertain to boxing, even if he did not agree with the laws. In his deposition, he had stated that he had charged me double the statutory amount of the bond because, in his words, "It's not *my* fault that there's more money in the white pocket than in the black pocket . . .That's not my concern . . . It was a question of whether we would allow any black promoters in Massachusetts...Not having any (black promoters in Massachusetts) was an option that I could have, and should have, exercised."

When asked about this comment, he said, "I was only being facetious."

I noted that if a white man had made the same statement, they would not be worrying about if the jury would see those words as racist, and hoped that they would measure him by his words and actions. He had no comment why there were no records in the Commission files of any white promoters needing to obtain a bond.

Harry had Brown restate the document that had been distributed. He asked him if he was positive of the events, and Brown insisted that he remembered it clearly. He said that they "just could not let him (Smith) run his event. He had broken the rules, and we couldn't let him proceed, the same as Zeke". Harry informed him that they would come back to that issue in a moment.

Step by step, Harry lead him back through the day's testimony, having him repeat and confirm his statements, and especially his letter stating that *"ignorance of the law is no excuse."* As he reviewed each of the Regulations of the Boxing Commission that were actually in effect in October and November of 1996, he referred to the documentation to show that there was not one instance where I broke any law or regulation.

After highlighting that there was no prescribed minimum of bouts for an event, Harry asked him about the bouts that were on the schedules that I provided to the Commission. Brown reiterated that his first priority was to have good bouts, so that the public would be entertained, and to make sure that the bouts were safe for all participants.

I had supplied Harry with all of the arguments and documentation he needed for cross-examination. In fact, the documentation was provided in the initial discovery packet that I had sent to the State years before. For each proposed bout, I listed each fighter's previous approved bouts, and the records of the fighters that they fought.

Without exception, the fighters proposed had fought under the Massachusetts Boxing Commission within six months of my event, and most of them within two months. As Harry asked him, bout by bout, for the reason that the fight was not good, Brown gave a reason—some were "not good fighters," some of them were "in process of having their licenses revoked," some of them he claimed "just could not fight."

And bout-by-bout, Harry used an easel stand and presentation sheets to demonstrate the records of the two fighters, and whom they had previously fought with the approval of the Commission.

Without exception, Cooper and Brown had approved the same fighters to compete against boxers with more dissimilar records than the ones that I had submitted, in events being held by white promoters. And all of the fighters who he claimed were in process of license suspension fought regularly since then.

They felt that they could misuse their authority to

prevent me from running my event by disallowing every bout I submitted, then invoking a non-existent "minimum bout" rule as an excuse to finally cancel the event. The mood was intense as Harry disproved every excuse Brown gave for the Commission's decision.

Then came the moment that would climax the entire cross-examination. While it seemed from the documents that Smith actually had not submitted his fight card within the allowed limits, Harry had already demonstrated to the jury that I submitted my fight card in plenty of time, but because Cooper did not approve the bouts, I had to keep substituting more fighters, which were again disallowed by Cooper.

This went on until the Commission finally cancelled the event for "not having enough bouts."

About that time, the jury was listening intently. Harry brought Brown back to the issue with Smith, and asked him if there was any change in his testimony. Brown assured him that he was positive in his memory, and besides, the documents that Kapinski handed to the jury proved that they cancelled the event.

A hush fell over the Defendants and Kapinski as

Harry stood and faced the jury for just a moment. He turned and handed Brown a sheet of paper and asked him to identify the signature at the bottom of the page.

Brown hesitated, then cleared his throat and replied, "It's my signature." After entering the document into evidence, Harry asked him to identify the heading on the form. The jury listened intently as Brown identified the form as the Event Form that he was required to send to *Fight Fax,* a nationwide boxing report service, after each and every event held in Massachusetts.

Harry asked Brown to identify which event this particular report was prepared for, and Brown identified the event as the one held by Smith, the same event that he had repeatedly sworn was cancelled, and the one concerning which the Defense had distributed the manufactured document to the jurors.

A murmur went through the courtroom. By the end of the day, Brown had admitted that the Commissioners could cite no valid reason for interfering with my event, that not only did he testify falsely but caused a fabricated document to be distributed to the jury.

With that statement, Harry concluded his cross-examination and the court recessed until Friday.

◆————————◆

First thing Friday morning, Kapinski called as his next witness, Paul Johnson, who testified that as a black man, he had never had occasion to experience any discrimination in connection with a boxing event in the Commonwealth. He was obviously well prepared for his testimony, and painted a picture of Commissioners who live to serve the promoters and fighters under their authority.

As he finished, Harry smiled once more. During the recess, I was sitting in the courtroom and could hear Johnson arguing with Cooper, Brown, Kapinski and Patrick Reed. Apparently, they were paying him to testify and told him that he would be scheduled for Thursday. Because he had to come back an additional day he was trying to increase the amount of the payment. The Defense had not disclosed this information, and I'm sure that they would have preferred for the Court not to be aware of the payment.

Harry asked him to confirm and reconfirm a

summary of his testimony, making sure that the jury understood him precisely—making sure he was clear about his memories of the circum-stances. Then, Harry produced the award report from a discrimination complaint that Johnson had filed with the State, and which the state had found and awarded in his favor. Johnson looked stunned, but not half as much as Kapinski did.

I wondered what would prompt a black man, who had himself experienced discrimination while running events, and who had found it necessary to also take action and knew how difficult it was to prove, to get on the stand and testify under oath in support of the same treatment he complained about.

I'm sure that he was under tremendous pressure from the Commission, because his license had been suspended indefinitely by the Boxing Commission, and he did admit that he was being paid for his appearance when Harry asked.

After we proved the State's initial two witnesses as liars, Kapinski next called Barbara Jones, Event Coordinator for the Madison Park Community Center, who testified that I left without paying for the facility I had arranged. Ms. Jones' testimony was brief, and Harry quickly provided a letter, which she identified, written by her boss.

The letter clarified that there was no money owing as a result of the cancelled event, and she confirmed that she did receive a copy of the letter from him. Ms. Jones was quickly excused after she testified that she had written her letter after Cooper called her numerous times and prompted her to write a letter of complaint to the Commission, promising that he would make sure that "he (Zeke) never runs a show in our state again."

Next, it was time for Cooper to take the stand. He spoke about his background, and his service to the community as a member of the Brookline Police Department. He spoke about his love of boxing and the career that his brother had in the sport.

Cooper insisted, despite all evidence to the contrary, that I broke all of the rules of the Commission. He didn't have too much else to say, and his cross-examination was brief. His testimony was highlighted by the fact that he did not deny his conversation with George Taylor. By now, it was well into the day on Friday, and court recessed until Monday morning, when the attorneys would offer final arguments before turning the outcome over to the jury.

It had now been three weeks since I came to Boston for a one-hour pretrial conference. I was afraid to go home for the weekends, because my aging van might not make another trip home and back, and I could not afford to miss Court on Monday morning.

I had depleted my checking account early in the trial preparation week, and had called my sister Frenisee, who wired me the three hundred dollars that my family was using for meals and transportation costs. Needless to say, now looking at the weekend, one more day of court, and waiting for the jury's decision, I was once again running low on cash.

Connie's father had arranged to put the motel room on his credit card, so we didn't have to worry about a place to stay. We spent the weekend resting and waiting. Exciting as it was, the week of court had been exhausting, and we found ourselves spending Saturday in our room.

On Sunday, we visited a local church and afterward took Flo to a nearby park to enjoy the early autumn sunshine and to pass the time. I had received a small paycheck from my job as a youth counselor by direct deposit, and I figured out, with my remaining cash, how much I would need for gas to return home, an estimate of another five days of traveling back and forth to the city, and money for food.

It was going to be close, and we wondered if we could do it.

We were still at the park, watching Flo play and looking over our budget, when Connie came upon some money lying in the grass, far away from the paved walking paths.

It was odd, almost as if it had been placed there on purpose. The money was folded neatly, and was completely dry in spite of the fact that there had been a light rain that morning. For the few hours that we had been there, no one else visited that end of the park. Two people could not have been more grateful for twenty-seven dollars. Connie and I took it as a sign that, once again, we would get what we needed.

Monday morning came, and both attorneys delivered their final arguments, doing their best to take one final opportunity to make an impression on the minds of the jurors. Notably, Harry pointed out that Cooper never denied George's allegation. He asked the jurors if that wouldn't be the first thing that they would do if the accusation was false—and I saw a lot of the jurors nod their heads in agreement.

Harry also reminded the jury that when he asked Brown if he felt that I was treated fairly, Brown paused for about ten seconds, then replied, "I guess the way we treated him was wrong."

When both sides rested, Chief Justice Travis gave the jury instructions. He explained that they would now have the job of weighing the testimony, the facts presented, and to decide in the case of conflicting testimony which side was telling the truth.

He explained that this was a case in which they should put the merits of each side on an imaginary scale, and to find for the party who the scale tips toward. He also instructed them that should they find unanimously for the Plaintiff, only then would they need to come to an agreement on the amount of award to be given in two separate categories; compensatory damages to compensate for actual loss sustained by the Plaintiff, and punitive damages against either or both Defendants separately, according to the degree of involvement in the wrongful activity.

However, he went on to explain that should they find for the Defendants, they would be excused, and should some of them find for the Defendant and some of them for the Plaintiff, then the trial would end with a verdict for the Defendants.

As the jurors retired to the jury room, I felt confident yet nervous, excited and afraid at the same time. The entire case was now in the hands of these twelve men and women.

And the waiting began. As the day ended, and the second day began, Harry explained that this was a good sign. He asked me, "Are you ready for day eight?"

I replied, "It's only the Eighth Round. We'll see what the day brings."

Because of the issues involved, we needed a unanimous verdict, not just a majority. Harry told me that the time that had passed indicated to him that the jurors were all in agreement, and were now in the process of deciding the amount of the award.

Kapinski must have agreed, because it was then that he approached me with an offer of one hundred thousand dollars.

Harry nodded and smiled as I reminded Kapinski that it had been four years since I sought the state's help in resolving this issue. After four years of financial harm, two years of pleadings, surviving a pro se deposition, multiple motions to dismiss, a summary judgment, and a week of trial, not one of my facts had changed, not one of my opinions changed, and I had remained reasonable and followed the prescribed system for trying to set things straight.

I told him that, having come that far, "I would rather take a dime from the jury than to take a hundred thousand dollars from the State."

And we continued to wait.

Finally, at about 1:30 in the afternoon, the jury reached their decision. The courtroom clerk walked through the hallway, announcing, "Wilson versus Brown, the jury will return their verdict in fifteen minutes."

I felt an instant rush of emotion as I made my way

to the courtroom. Kapinski was already there, and was no longer taunting me with opinions of how the verdict would be—he was now predicting the award. It seems as if, out of nowhere, there was a sudden rush of people into the audience of the courtroom, and as an army all had risen for the judge to enter.

It's amazing how things seem to move in slow motion when adrenaline is pumping. I watched as the jury seemed to enter in slow motion and take their places in the jury box. I watched as the judge asked the forewoman if the jury had reached a verdict. She indicated that they had. When the judge asked her to read the verdict, she paused, and announced, "We the jury find unanimously for the Plaintiff and against the Defendants."

A wave of emotion moved through the courtroom. I had to sit down, very happy that justice had prevailed after all. Harry, Denise and Connie were ecstatic. As I sat down, I could see Flo jumping up and down.

The next morning, I once again returned to Pennsylvania as I did almost four years before, but this time I was far from being exhausted and angry.

Connie and Flo Wilson, September 2000

ACKNOWLEDGEMENT

◆————————◆

First and foremost, I would like to give thanks to God and to the Lord Jesus Christ.

I would also love to give thanks to my Mother, Mrs. Florence H. Wilson, who instilled in me a will to go on and never give up.

I would like to give thanks to my sister Frenisee Wilson-West for helping me in everything I try to do.

I would like to thank my youngest sister, Vernell Wilson LeGree, for being my time-keeper when I first got started.

I would also like to thank my Uncle Rufus and Aunt Jenna for helping me see my way.

I'd also like to give a special thanks to the guys who I trained with or were an influence in my life--Charles Singleton, Marvis Frazier, Joe Frazier, Leon Spinks, Randall "Tex" Cobb, Tim Witherspoon, James Broad, Ron Lyles, Jimmy Young, Ken Norton, Gerry Cooney, Gil Murrell, Richard Kates, Larry Holmes, Jake Lamotta, Rocky Graciano, Gene Tunney, Duane Bobick, Michael Spinks, Muhammad Ali, Jerry Quarry, George Foreman, Michael Moorer, Tommy Hearns, Mike Tyson, David Bey, Tony Tubbs and Evander Holyfield.

I would also like to give thanks to boxing trainers and managers who influenced my life, including Macauley Washburn, Sgt. David "Top" Robinson, Willie Folks, Eddie Futch, Emile Griffith, Emmanuel Stewart, Richard Giachetti, Cus D'Amato, Angelo Dundee and Archie Moore.

I would like to give special thanks to Steve DePass, Robert Guillaume, Norman Henry, John Connelly, Eugene Connelly, Chuck Donaldson, Joe Sirola, John Condon, Paul DiAmico and Robert Baran, who gave me help and guidance with my pro career.

I would like to give special thanks to my attorneys, Harvey Schwartz, Kim Sheckner,   and   Anthony

Giannascoli; special thanks to Cliff Phippen and to my wife, Connie Wilson, and my daughter Florence M. Wilson.

I'd also like to give a special thanks to all of the men and women I served with in the United States Marine Corps, especially the guys who served with me on the Marine Corps Boxing Team, and my artillery units at Camp Pendleton and Twenty-Nine Palms, California.

Special thanks to all of the Red Cross volunteers who I served with during the Hurricane Katrina disaster.

I would like to give thanks to all of the men and women of the USA Amateur Athletic Union, past and present.

I'd like to thank all of the people in Frogmore /Beaufort, South Carolina who believed in my ability to do more.

I'd like to thank all of the friends I encountered in Philadelphia and Los Angeles who believed in me. Special thanks to my friends, Dennis Murphy and Lance Freeman.

Special thanks to the folks at
Punch Out Publishing.
Their dedication to this project
made it possible.
You can visit them online at
http://www.punchoutpublishing.com

*"Providing literature that makes
a lasting impact."*

"The liberties of our country, the freedom of our civil
Constitution, are worth defending at all hazards; and it is
our duty to defend them against all attacks. We have
received them as a fair inheritance from our worthy
ancestors: they purchased them for us with toil and danger
and expense of treasure and blood, and transmitted them
to us with care and diligence. It will bring an everlasting
mark of infamy on the present generation, enlightened as
it is, if we should suffer them to be wrested from us by
violence without a struggle, or to be cheated out of them
by the artifices of false and designing men."
Samuel Adams

About the Author

Zeke Wilson was born in Frogmore, SC the seventh of eight children. In 1973 he began his boxing career and was trained by Macauley Washburn and the All-Marine Boxing Champion Sgt. David Robinson.

Wilson used his boxing skills to earn many honors during his amateur career. In November of 1975, he fought David Thompson in Hilton Head, SC for the South Carolina State Championship. He also won the South Carolina Golden Gloves in 1975. Upon graduating from Beaufort High School in 1976, Zeke relocated to Philadelphia, PA and trained under the tutelage of George Benton and the former World Heavyweight Champion Joe Frazier.

His amateur accomplishments qualified him to compete in the USA AAU (Amateur Athletic Union) Heavyweight Box-off held in June of 1977. He won the Heavyweight Elimination held in the Riverfront Coliseum in Cincinnati, OH, which qualified him for a seat on the US Boxing Team. As his experience in the sport grew, he enlisted in the US Marine Corps and became a member of the Marine Corps boxing team. In July of 1980, he competed successfully in the Marine Base Championship at Camp Pendleton, CA.

After serving four years in the Marine Corps, Zeke was honorably discharged with a Good Conduct Medal and a Meritorious Mass. One week later, he had his pro debut in Madison Square Garden. Just one month later, he became a sparring partner for then-current World Heavyweight Champion Larry Holmes. His career continued to advance, and in addition to fighting on a pro-fessional level he also formed Wilson Promotional Group and MW Productions to train, manage and promote both amateur and professional prize-fighters.

Wilson developed an aerobic boxing program, called Ze'Box, to answer the basic fitness needs of people of all ages and physical conditions. The guiding philosophy of Big Zeke's Fitness is that fitness is not defined by size or weight, but it means being able to exert yourself without feeling uncomfortable. The Ze'Box program is a low-impact, full-body workout that helps improve stamina, muscle tone, coordination and balance, and teach self-defense. You can visit his website at www.bigzekesfitness.com.

Zeke also enjoys weight training and various sports and physical activities. He has held state, national and world records in AAU Powerlifting, and currently serves as AAU Pennsylvania State Chairman of the Powerlifting program. He was honored by becoming the recipient of the AAU 2005 Youth Coach of the Year Award.

Zeke enjoys volunteering with the American Red Cross and recently served the population of New Orleans immediately following Hurricane Katrina by distributing food and supplies directly to members of the population still trapped in the city after the disaster.

He also serves as the Executive Director of a non-profit organization, Big Zeke's Power Kids, which provides growth opportunities and encourages a drug-free lifestyle for kids. You can visit their site at www.bigzekespowerkids.org

Zeke volunteers a good deal of time in counseling juveniles and helping them to see the necessity of setting goals and working to attain them.

Zeke has two children, Marcus and Florence, and currently lives in Pennsylvania with his wife, Connie, and his daughter, Florence.

Dear Reader,

If you find that this book has helped you to see the issue of justice from a new perspective,

If you have found from this book that you have the strength to face injustice in all of its forms,

Or, if reading this book has entertained you and fortified your courage,

Please recommend it to all of your friends, and ask them to pass the recommendation on! You can help to build a pyramid of people who demand "liberty and justice for all"!

--Zeke Wilson

The Eighth Round
is available online through
www.PunchOutPublishing.com,
or through your
favorite book retailer.
